Catering Complete

Booklocker.com, Inc.
2002

Catering Complete

Doug Pinkston

Thanks must go to my brother, Buddy Pinkston, who assisted with the copy editing of Catering Complete, and my friends and family, who have provided encouragement and support in this pursuit.

Table of Contents

Introduction

This book is a concise and complete guide to the procedural aspects of managing a catering operation. Too often books on catering focus on only one part of the puzzle----food preparation, say, or buffet design, or maybe even cost analysis----while providing very little useful information about the rest of the catering puzzle. Catering Complete provides a complete picture of the many pieces that must come together to manage a successful catering operation. You will find in this book answers to many questions. For example:

How can I maximize my sales investment?

Tried and true methods for producing professional portfolios are provided, along with methods for developing leads and getting the maximum exposure in your targeted markets.

How can I be sure I'm pricing my product correctly?

Catering Complete will provide you with specific step-by-step systems for determining menu and event pricing, along with the details of finalizing guest counts, guarantees and billing.

How do I find and keep professional employees?

The latest ideas in personnel recruiting, hiring and management are discussed, with ideas for organizing and utilizing an employee database.

What are the keys to running an effective and cost-efficient kitchen?

Food purchasing and inventory control measures are detailed, as well as methods for organizing your stock, developing your staff, and keeping food cost under budget.

How can I set large or intricate room sets quickly and without confusion?

Numerous specific systems for setting banquets are presented, along with an analysis of their uses and drawbacks.

How can I be sure my banquet service is better than the competition?

A complete discussion of contemporary styles of banquet service is provided, with specific service techniques that will help you provide that extra level of polish.

How do I organize my beverage department to control waste and theft?

Modern systems for managing your beverage costs are presented, as well as a quick primer of bar and wine service.

How do I put together a coffee service operation that can handle high-volume shows?

Numerous systems are presented for the staging and expediting of coffee breaks so you can meet all your service and cost projections.

How much equipment do I need, and how can I control breakage and theft?

Equipment purchasing, inventory management and systems for reducing loss and breakage are discussed, with specific suggestions on controlling your equipment and supply expenses.

How can I keep expenses in line with my sales?

Financial analysis tools are presented for computing product cost, labor costs, event budgeting and monthly cost statements.

Planning, Teamwork and Details

In 1996 I held the position as the Manager of the Executive Suites and Hosted Services at the Georgia Dome, in Atlanta. You may remember that in the summer of 1996 Atlanta hosted the Centennial Olympic Games. The scale, complexity and quality standards of our role made it imperative that we be thoroughly prepared for this massive event. Both basketball and gymnastics were scheduled to take place in our stadium. The plan was to create two stadiums out of one by separating the building with a curtain across the fifty-yard line. The individual events were scheduled to ping pong back and forth, with three or four separate ticketed events every day, for 20 days straight. To make the math even more difficult, the daily schedules did not follow a consistent pattern. One day you might have basketball, gymnastics, basketball; and on the next basketball, gymnastics, gymnastics. We serviced 100 suites on each venue, with an average of 20 people per suite. On our advance menu we sold 43 distinct buffet offerings, along with an expansive a la carte menu and beverage list. In addition, we offered an order-today-for-tomorrow menu and event-day snacks and beverages. In numerous other areas on the property we hosted meals and parties from dawn to midnight. Needless to say, it was catering on a scale that none of us could have imagined. We began our planning for the summer games more than a year out, adapting our specific procedures as event schedules, menus, Olympic Committee requests and requirements, and hundreds of other contingencies were, one-by-one, finalized. We hired over 400 employees for my department alone. Eventually, of course, the doors did open and we pulled together as a team to welcome the world. I can't tell you that everything went perfectly. But we did manage to pull it off. In fact, after a few days, things settled down into a somewhat comfortable pattern of operations. Our guests were pleased with our efforts and left our site with positive experiences.

I recount this story to make a simple point: Good planning and teamwork can accomplish some amazing things. In this book I have tried to focus on the planning aspects of managing a catering operation, as well as passing on a few thoughts on how to engender teamwork. Having spent 20 years in food service management----much of it in high-volume, high profile catering operations----I have been exposed to numerous systems and approaches for managing the many tasks that confront the professional caterer.

I have tried to bring the best of these systems together in an easy-to-understand, logical format which should provide a great resource for anyone considering the start-up of a catering business, students studying the subject for course work, or for established catering professionals at all levels. While there are many general concepts and ideas presented, I have focused on specific procedures as much as possible. A quality catering operation (like any other business) depends on how well all the little details are managed. Developing and documenting step-by-step procedures is always the first step in the process. You will notice that in almost every chapter there are specific ideas for using a computer to make your business more efficient. Catering is a business filled with great amounts of constantly changing information. How well you manage this information will play a big part in how well you manage your entire operation. At the end of this book I have included numerous forms, checklists and diagrams that I believe you will find helpful. These are referenced as they are mentioned in each chapter.

Space, Time and Continuity

In any operation, but particularly in an operation involving as many unique and disparate elements as a banquet, it is important to understand how each element affects the others. Planning decisions do not exist in a vacuum. A plan works or doesn't work as it fits in with the entire flow of the event. Thus, you must consider each aspect of a banquet, not in isolation, but in the context of its impact on all other considerations. In addition, banquets take place in real space and time, with real people. You must take into account how your guests *and your employees* flow through the space and time of the event if you are to set up and service a functional and successful banquet. Often, this piece of the planning process is the most difficult. If you could just feed everybody in the kitchen (off the prep tables, say) your job would be a lot easier. But clients tend to be picky!

You will notice a continual reference to how a part of the banquet flows within the entire banquet. Indeed, the chapters in this book flow----in chronological order----through the various stages of a banquet----from selling, to planning, to production, to breakdown and finally, financial analysis. As I will show you, many mistakes can be avoided just by keeping the concept of flow foremost in your mind.

The polished caterer is able to envision the flow of an event (from beginning to end) before the first fork is set. It is the ability to anticipate and plan for possible bottlenecks in the preparation and service of a banquet that is the key to pulling off a polished event. The old adage----put yourself in the client's shoes----is never more apt than in catering. You must constantly attempt to strike a balance between flash, function and financial viability. If I could leave any banquet manager with any one idea or concept, it would be: Remember the Flow!

Chapter 1

Sales, Marketing and Event Planning

In general, everything that has ever been said about sales can also be said about the art of selling a banquet. All the techniques that apply to selling software, shoes or hay apply equally to catering sales. While there are limitless approaches and strategies for managing the sales process, selling well is no real mystery. Much of it boils down to perseverance, organizational skills and a little bit of personality. There is no question that some individuals are just naturally much better at this craft than others. It is often true in the food business that many who enjoy the art of cooking are not as comfortable in the art of serving. And some who enjoy serving clients are not particularly good at convincing them to make a purchase. So you must be sure that whoever is assigned the sales function is the right person for the job. Your sales staff must combine a pleasant nature, unbelievable patience, good administrative skills and the ability to convince a complete stranger to do things the way you want them done; at your price. Of these skills, the first two are probably the most valuable.

But generating sales in a catering operation is much more than just being bubbly and informed. In order to formalize the process of attracting and keeping clients, caterers must qualify and quantify their approach. Having the best food and service in the world means nothing, of course, if you can't get the customer to experience it. Let us examine a few specific ideas on how to approach the sales function and some hard and fast rules on how to sell the event.

1. Define Your Market

The first step in any marketing program is to do a full and detailed analysis of who your potential clients are in the local marketplace. Where are they located? Are they business or residential? Are they large or small? Are they high budget or lower end? Do you do weddings or Bar Mitzvahs? It is appropriate to get as much information as you can about who your competition is and what they are doing. The first order of business would be too simply call ever caterer in the phone book and have them mail you a copy of their menus. Ask about what types of events they specialize in and what clients they have hosted recently. Understanding your competition better enables you to present your relative strengths and to play down your weaknesses.

If, like most firms, you are targeting several markets at once, it may make sense to segment your marketing strategies and/or staff. Many firms divide their sales staff by corporate or private catering, or even by specific types of functions, such as weddings, receptions, dinners or special entertainment-related events. By allowing your sales associates to stay focused in a particular area they gain greater expertise and familiarity with all the particulars of their assignment.

Within these market considerations it is useful to also define your particular areas of expertise. What types of events are you best at, and thus, where is your competitive advantage over the competition. For example, if you cannot profitably handle large functions (in the 500-person range, say), then you may want to eliminate these clients from your target list. On the other hand, if your firm has the facilities and expertise to put on elegant wedding receptions then that segment of the market should be targeted for an appropriate amount of sales resources.

When I worked at the Georgia World Congress Center we had the largest ballroom in Atlanta (seating 2000 comfortably for dinner) and exhibit halls where we could sit over 10,000. This clearly gave us a monopoly on any very large group that wanted to put on a formal function. Of course, any convention group in residence was always a ready target for our sales efforts. Often, simply your proximity to particular churches, arenas, meeting halls and entertainment complexes present natural opportunities.

2. Developing and Managing Leads

All your analysis and strategizing ultimately must be turned into something tangible and money producing. The first step in closing in a sale is generating a lead. It has been proven that the most successful salespeople are those who aggressively develop and pursue leads. This is an area where sheer volume pays off. You should put in place a client database, containing not just names and addresses, but any information you can dig up, including every contact you have had with the potential customer, every event you have hosted for them, and any miscellaneous comments that a salesperson may feel is relevant to a future sale. The more information you have readily available the better you will be able to anticipate and meet your client's needs.

It will be your goal to expand your client list. This will be done through lead referrals, advertising and – sometimes -- aggressive cold calling. Work your leads like your job depended on it (as, of course, it does). The most successful salespeople are not the ones with the flashiest smiles, or most elegant presentations, but simply the ones who are the most persistent. Pay close attention to what conventions and groups are coming to town as far in advance as you can gather the information. If particular trade shows or conventions visit your area on a regular basis, subscribe to their journals and look at the possibility of advertising there. I've seen salespeople go as far as to walk through the local hotels, checking the banquet postings in an effort to get a feel for what different groups were doing in the local market.

You should use your current bookings to develop new ones. The key to developing leads is through networking your existing contacts. Whenever you do a large or distinctive function for a trade or business group, you can send an account of the event to the associated trade publications, along with photos. If the client is happy with your event you should try to get a few good words of recommendation as well. In some cases you might want to ask if you could use their words of reference in your sales catalogues or brochures. Be sure to add all influential attendees of your functions to your database. There is nothing wrong with a follow-up correspondence to someone who may have just been introduced to at a banquet you are hosting. You should make it hard for your customers to forget that you want their business and you appreciate it. Make it difficult for them to ever contract with another caterer. The most important asset any company has is its reputation. Protect it and promote it vigorously.

3. Managing Information

How well you manage information will play a crucial role in how well you attract and keep customers. Nothing is more frustrating for a client than working with a firm that cannot keep precise records on the specific details of your events. In addition, the speed and ease with which you can put together your proposals, contracts and event orders can have a direct impact on your bottom line. There are numerous software systems available to help you manage the entire marketing function. Here are a few of the features of one prominent provider:

- Automated event books that eliminates double bookings and make it easy to check space, change information, and move or duplicate event reservations.

- Unique entry system, which follows the natural flow of scheduling an event. You really can input order information while you talk to the customer.

- The ability to produce custom event orders, confirmation letters and proposals in minutes.

- A trace system that automatically tracks every action required for an event. It's easy to check an event's progress and manage daily tasks.

- A "customer call screen" with a history of all customer communication, eliminating the need for handwritten notes.

- Change orders, automatically generated when a change is made to an event order already distributed to other departments.

- Financial tools to track deposit and payment information, summarize revenue, and generate invoices and banquet checks.

- Reports and graphs for rapid checks of forecasted revenues and salesperson performance.

- Unique systems for managing group events that require individual reservations.

- Integrated software, linking "off-the-menu" events with the Dining Reservations module to avoid over booking and improve communication.

Now that sounds like a caterer's dream system. But a system like that is not cheap. And it takes a considerable amount of time and training to get it up and running and to realize its potential. Nevertheless, it is clear that the caterer who makes use of technology, particularly in their marketing efforts, has a distinct advantage over the caterer who relies on the more traditional methods of managing information, such as files of memos, letters and handwritten notes.

4. Marketing, Advertising and PR

Very few firms have the budget to spend large amounts of money on advertising, whether in local periodicals, on billboards, or in other media. Thus, you must make use of marketing approaches that are more clever than expensive. Some ongoing investment in advertising is necessary to be sure your name gets the proper exposure in the local marketplace, but many marketing concepts can be put in to place for a minimum of expense.

You should start with your portfolio. It's a good idea to purchase a high quality camera (with a tripod), and to take shots of every unique or distinctive event that you host. You may even find a staff member whose hobby is photography that will do the work cheaply just for the resume experience. (Hiring professionals can sometimes be more expensive than TV, and even less useful). Using these photos you should develop a set of catalogues that include bios of your chef and management team, along with a selection of your better menus. Your catalogues can be displayed in the office, as well as taken with you on sales calls. This gives the client real-life examples of the quality of your work, and may also provide them with some menu and presentation ideas. Select your best photos to use in brochures or mailings. I don't know if a picture is worth a thousand words, but it's definitely better than a bunch of flowery descriptions.

It is clearly a necessity in today's market to have a web presence as well. Websites can be put together for a minimal expense and can provide tremendous impact and exposure. The web is often the first place that people look when searching for particular products or services. It is certainly the simplest and most efficient method of communicating with your potential customers. By including a broad portfolio on your websites you can feature the best of your efforts. It never hurts to include numerous shots of your guests enjoying themselves as well. A picture, in this case, could mean a thousand dollars.

The key to developing leads is through connections. Whenever you do a large or distinctive function for a trade or business group, you can send an account of the event to the associated trade publications, along with photos. If the client is happy with your event you should try to get a few good words of recommendation as well. In some cases you might want to ask if you can use their words of reference in your sales catalogues or brochures. The most valuable advertising tool in the world is word of mouth.

Always follow up every event with thank-you letters. It is perfectly acceptable in such a letter to pitch proposals for other events that the client may be planning in the future. Be sure you place flags in your data base system to remind you of any such events. Look at every event as an opportunity to establish a long-term relationship with the client. Your job is to convince them that you can provide them with the best banquet at the best price, and there is no longer any need for them to shop around.

Attracting the client, however, is only part of what a good salesperson should accomplish. They must guide the client through the process of determining all the details of their event, and pass this information on to the kitchen and operations staff in a format they can interpret and execute. Let us look at the proper way to put a banquet together.

5. Menu Planning

There is one thing you can probably determine about every client from the outset: *They enjoy food!* With very few exceptions everyone likes to eat. This is part of what makes catering (and food service) so enjoyable: You're able to witness first-hand a pleasurable reaction to your efforts in one of life's most pleasurable activities. This doesn't mean, however, that everyone has the same tastes. Determining what will be served at a banquet is often, but not always, the most important decision that is made.

Your first objective, when planning a menu, must be to pick items your guests will enjoy. Remember that your client----the one paying the bill---is only one palate of many (if the client even attends the event). Ultimately, it is the enjoyment of the attendees that will determine the banquet's success. A gorgeous display of ostrich pates and wild hare terrines (sculpted into the shape of the honoree, say), may bring your client----and even yourself----to culinary ecstasy, but if it sits in the corner barely picked at, then you've blown it! Your job as a salesperson is to guide the client to select a menu their guests will enjoy. Always ask the question: Who will actually attend the banquet and what do they like?

Though occasionally clients will come to you who have a firm idea of what they would like to have served at their event, most clients expect you, as the expert, to guide them to an informed decision. Obviously, you will start by letting them review your printed menus, and having a look at your portfolio. Guiding them towards established menus is always the recommended track when it can be accomplished, but don't be afraid to accept their ideas. I have a rather simple approach to dealing with client suggestions. If it is possible to do without undue price or logistical implications then I agree to it. It's that simple. It is their buck and their party. Give them ownership. A common mistake made by catering salespeople is to feel as if they own the party, not the client, and the whole planning process ends up being a tug-of-war. No one likes to be shot down out of hand, no matter how poor his or her suggestion. And remember: anything can be done, as long as the client is willing to pay for it.

On those occasions when the client does suggest an idea fraught with challenges you must approach the situation carefully. I always begin by shaking my head approvingly and complimenting them on their idea. After a moment I will slowly bring my objections to light, as though they are coming to me as I more carefully consider their proposal. "That's a good idea," I might say. "I'm wondering though: if we served such a large salad, would that make them less like to enjoy the rest of the dinner that we're planning." (Secretly, you know that you would to have rent large salad plates for the dish the client has in mind.) "Have you seen the picture of our chef's Waldorf salad? This would make a great impression as a first course." As always, the secret to keeping everyone happy is compromise.

6. Work With Your Kitchen

When working with the client to develop a menu it is critical that the salesperson understands the capabilities and expertise of the kitchen staff. Your printed menus will always provide the most obvious suggestions. Over time, your kitchen staff will have developed an expertise with these items. It is likely, in fact, that one or more members of your kitchen management staff developed the current menu. A simple dish prepared superbly will bring many more smiles than an exotic dish that falls short.

It is appropriate to introduce your client to one or more of your chef's during the planning stages. This being the case, it is also appropriate to be sure your chef's wear professional culinary uniforms when on the premises. In the same way, a clean and orderly kitchen is a necessity. Many clients will request a walk-through of the premises before signing the contract.

You should involve the culinary staff in the menu planning process as much as possible. Your kitchen staff will always be the experts on food and production. Their involvement in the menu planning stages will enrich the process with their expertise and also allow you to better consider logistical and budgetary considerations. You must strive to keep cost and price in balance.

7. Know Your Space

Very few clients have enough experience with catering to know how many people will fit into a certain size space. Your experience and training must guide them. If your client is determined to put a 500-person banquet into a space that only holds 400, then you've got a problem. I can't think of anything that will ruin a banquet faster and more completely than poor space planning. We all know the experience of showing up at what we thought would be a gala evening, only to find ourselves crushed into an ice carving or an empty dessert buffet, with no hope of making it to the bar.

Most firms allow the banquet operations managers to develop and/or finalize any large or unusual room sets. Generally, they will have more experience in dealing with the details of making a layout work, and ultimately they are the ones who must set the room and serve the guests. Just as you consult with the chef as you develop and finalize your menu, you should consult with the banquet manager as you develop and finalize your room sets.

Always walk your client through the space in use during the function, either physically or by diagram, and explain any potential problems with their ideas. People need a certain amount of space to feel comfortable and they tend to move around (thus, there is a *flow* to their movement). It is preferable to be forceful, but courteous, on the front side, rather than embarrassed and apologetic later.

8. Know Your Costs

Everything costs money. The successful caterers will always be those who can balance the sale of the event with its cost. An understanding of your own budget (along with the clients) will help you to devise menu plans that will keep everyone happy and your firm profitable. Planning and pulling off a beautiful and elaborate banquet that impresses everyone, but loses money, will be your showpiece only for a short while. Ultimately, it is profitability that will be the measure of your success.

Many catering operations require a cost analysis to be submitted before finalizing any contract. In the last chapter we will look more closely at financial analysis and budgeting for profitability.

9. Details, Details

As you put together the details of your event, always imagine the *flow* of your guests through the space from the beginning to the end. You should have a detailed knowledge of when the guests will be arriving. For example: Are they driving in their own cars? Are they coming from home or work? Are they arriving by bus, train, or charter? Are there other events before or after yours? If your guests arrive a few at a time, a few well-maintained bars and buffets may work nicely. If all 300 arrive at once, however, you will need more points of service and they will need to be spread out.

In addition to the timing of your guests' arrival, it's important to consider the length of the function. If a group only has an hour to eat and run, you will need a different service approach (more buffets or more servers, or both) than if the event is spread out over two hours. Presentations, speeches and room displays will also affect how your guests will flow through the room. Try to imagine the logical flow of the entire group within the time and space constraints of the event, and design your service strategies accordingly. A thorough checklist, encompassing all the important details of an event, is helpful and, for new salespeople, indispensable. I've included a sample checklist in the addendum.

10. Guarantees, Sets and Billing

As you meet with your clients to finalize the details of your event you will need to have the client sign off on the number of people you will serve and the specific quantities of food and beverages you will provide. With a seated (plated) meal, you will have to establish the total meals the client expects and agrees to pay for.

Generally, seated functions are sold with a guarantee count and a set count. The guarantee is a guaranteed number of guests the caterer will set and serve and that the client has agreed (by contract), to pay for---- regardless of how many people actually eat. The set is generally a certain cushion beyond the guarantee (often 5%), which the caterer agrees to set and prepare for in the event that a few extra show up. Any extra meals are charged to the client based on the actual count beyond the guarantee. Some caterers specify that any change in the guarantee within 24 hours automatically changes the guarantee count to the set count and the client will be billed accordingly.

It is a good rule to follow to never set a single setting more than what the client has agreed to pay for (i.e. the set). Remember that your service staff assignments and your kitchen are all tied into the set count. Just because you set a few extra tables does not mean the kitchen will have meals prepared, or you will have staff to service them. It will, however, give the client that impression. All clients have a vested interest in keeping the guarantee count as close to the actual count as possible. They can "nickel and dime" you to death with set changes if you don't establish firm rules.

For buffets and receptions (essentially the same thing), you will either charge by the guest count or by the piece. Charging by the piece means you agree to provide and set out a specific quantity of specified items. If the client decides they need----or want----more, then they will be billed for the additions (providing the chef has not left for the night and your cupboard is not bare). A reception that is billed by the piece generally does not have a set count----only the agreed-upon quantities originally determined. It is good practice, however, to get from your chef a list of items available for replenishment in case the client decides to re-order.

When serving a meal buffet, clients are generally charged by the person. A plate count should be taken before and after the function to determine the number actually served. Meal buffets often will have a guarantee and a set count, billed in the same manner as a seated function.

It is conventional to require at least 50% payment at the time the contract is finalized. The remainder may be paid at the conclusion of the event, or billed by invoice. Obviously, any changes in the guest count, or product being offered, should be sent to the client in writing and confirmed by signature. It is a good practice to have the client sign off on even the most minor of changes. This aids greatly in preventing any surprises (and potentially last minute changes), on event day.

At the conclusion of each function you should have a lead captain, supervisor, banquet manager, or salesperson, present the Banquet Event Order (or Function Sheet, or Contract) to the client for signature. The actual number served should be clearly written on the form as well as any additions or replenishments to the product originally ordered. It is a good idea to use this opportunity to solicit specific feedback from the client, rather than just get a signature and disappear. Obviously, any complaints should be immediately communicated up the chain of command. You are better off to at least consider making some adjustments to the bill, particularly with a valued, unhappy client, than you are to take the attitude that a product served is a product paid for. Small adjustments here and there can make a big difference in a client's satisfaction and a firm's reputation.

11. Handling Guest Complaints

No one who has worked in the food service business for longer than a week has not had to deal with a customer complaint. It is as much a part of the business as washing the dishes. Like interviewing and counseling employees, experience helps in this subtle craft, but there are some guidelines that can help you make the most of a bad circumstance.

- Gather what information you can from your service staff. You don't want to be caught by surprise in such a delicate situation.

- Think ahead to what you can offer to make up for the shortfall. Some establishments allow for a generous comp policy. If a guest is unhappy you might comp the entire check. In other cases, a free drink is enough to win them over.

- Listen fully to your guest's remarks. One of the biggest mistakes managers make is to preempt the complaint by approaching the customer with a collection of apologies and excuses. If the problem has reached the stage of a formal complaint then the customer will not be satisfied until they are given a chance to air their grievance. Often you will find that what you perceived as the problem was entirely different than what the customer tells you.

- Don't make excuses. Always remember that you are dealing with a customer's perception of the situation, not necessarily the exact reality. If your customer has determined there is a problem, then you must deal with the problem, as they perceive it.

- Accept responsibility. Whatever it is that they are unhappy about the customer has already determined that it is your fault. The sooner you accept that fact the sooner you can move forward toward rectifying the shortcoming. I usually start by saying, "I apologize for (whatever it is that you are upset about)".

12. Hosted Versus Cash Bars

Whenever bars are required for a function you will have to determine whether the client prefers to have a hosted bar or a cash bar. A hosted bar means simply that the drinks are on the house and whatever is consumed will be paid for by the client. With a cash bar, on the other hand, the guests must pay for their own drinks. These budgetary decisions should be handled carefully. Sometimes it makes sense to have hosted bars for a portion of the event (say, before dinner), and cash bars for another portion (say, after dinner). In some cases, you may have a combination of hosted and cash bars at the same time for the same client. Their VIP's, for example, may have a hosted bar behind the stage, while the underlings must pay as they go.

The billing for a cash bar is rather straightforward, though most operations require a minimum of sales for each bar they place. This minimum is to cover labor expenses in setting up the additional bars. With a hosted bar an exact inventory of the beverage product consumed must be taken before and immediately after the event. Many disagreements have arisen on the different accounting methods used to determine this final figure, so use a system that can be administered by the staff on hand and easily reviewed by management and the client (if they wish). We will discuss some ideas on this in Chapter 6, Managing the Beverage Department.

13. Layout Planning

Once you have a feel on the timing of your guest's arrival and departure you can begin to plan the set-up of your room(s). Remember that the overall impact of an event is a combination of food quality, presentation and service, and the three are closely interrelated. A few rules of thumb concerning buffet planning should be helpful.

Full Meal Buffets

1. Provide one line of service for each 100 to 150 guests. (Depending on time allowance and space).

2. Set your beverage and dessert tables separate from the main buffets, or provide beverage and desert service in the room. This prevents bottlenecks on the main buffets.

3. Use rolled silver on the buffet whenever acceptable, particularly with large groups. This prevents guests' re-sitting at an already used space that is dirty and not set.

4. Set your buffets so that there is a linear flow from the entrance point through the service lines, to the seating area and, finally, out the door.

Reception Buffets

1. Provide at least one point of service (location to pick up plates), for every 50 guests.

2. Feature the most attractive or exotic items in prominent locations (though not near the door, or in narrow aisle ways).

3. Avoid placing bars near the front doors or the bathrooms, whenever possible.

4. Try to get a picture of the menu items and their placement as you select table designs and locations. Table set-up flows from the menu.

5. Draw out your table designs and locations in diagram form. This will help you to better see what you're planning and also provide a helpful communication tool for the service staff.

Chapter 2

Staffing

Successful businesses never lose focus on their people; they are far and away the most important assets of any organization. Without enough quality employees, even the best-designed plans in the world will never come to fruition. The best managers are always recruiting, hiring, training, coaching, developing, promoting, and counseling. In the food service business, probably more than any other, turnover is constant, and if you don't look for employees today (when it appears you are fully staffed), you'll be short-staffed tomorrow, when two of your folks move to Phoenix, your best cook goes to the competition for fifty cents more an hour, and you catch your lead bartender giving away cocktails. On the reverse side of the dilemma, any organization that finds itself short-staffed with un-trained, poor-quality employees, is doomed to failure, or at best, mediocrity. Without enough good people you enter the fight with one hand tied behind your back.

1. Recruiting

Unless your firm is quite small, recruiting quality employees must be part of your every-day activities. Too often firms wait until they are short-staffed and then by knee-jerk reaction post their un-noteworthy classified ad alongside the rest of the food service enterprises desperate for help. I have managed operations in numerous restaurants, hotels and catering operations and almost everyone one of them was short of staff when I first joined them. And they all made the same excuses: We cannot maintain proper staffing because the local pool of talent is either too good for this job, or not good enough. Wrong! Your first step in overcoming this excuse is to not except it. You must make a commitment not to be short-staffed. If you do this, and employ a few of the suggestions discussed in this chapter, the staffing problem can be solved. I have done it 100's of times.

Attracting prospective employees does not solve your problem, but it is the first step in the solution. Here are a few tried-and-true techniques for attracting quality employees.

- Network from existing employees. Most employees that are satisfied with their job will be happy to recommend your firm to their friends. Rather than prohibit fraternization, like a firm out of 1955, you should encourage welcoming friends, relatives and associates into your organization. What better way to create a team. (Faced with the challenge of hiring several hundred employees for the Super Bowl in 1992 and the Olympics in 1996, a networked database developed from our existing staff accomplished the job with plenty of recruits to spare.)

- Keep a posting of your positions at all local colleges and stay in communication with the administrators of their placement offices.

- Don't simply post ads, use your ads to sell the position and the firm. Explain in a creative way why someone would want to work for you. Play up the intangibles of the job, but focus on pay as well, if you are even 10 cents above the market.

- Always be on the lookout for employees. Handing out business cards to potential service employees should be a routine. Whenever an employee introduces you to someone they know take a moment to talk to them. Your job as a manager is to sell your operation as a superior place to work.

2. Keep Enough Folks!

We're always looking for good people! In the food service business this banner should be hung right at the front door. Whatever number of employees you think you need to run your operation effectively today, you should always have a few more than that to cover unexpected turnover. Since most employees in this business are part-time, or on a pool status, adding a few extra, as long as they understand the nature of their schedule, costs you very little, and it can cost you a lot if you find yourself short of staff. Being short of staff can affect you in the following ways: overtime expense, poor productivity, poor morale, poor guest service and, eventually, more turnover. Not the least consideration is the fact that it becomes more difficult to hold employees to high standards when the manager can't afford to lose them.

3. Train, Train, Train

Just as it must become a habit to hire on a continual basis, you must also focus on training as a daily routine. Use all spare moments between functions to conduct training sessions. I made it a routine to quiz my employees on the standards and procedures which I expected them to know and follow. This technique works particularly well in meetings and informal group gatherings. Peer pressure will help to motivate your staff to acquaint themselves with your standards.

Formal training sessions should also be made part of your ongoing schedule. Treat these training sessions as though you were preparing a seminar for other managers, with professionally looking, up-to-date documents, props and facilities. Utilize your supervisor staff in smaller training groups. When dealing with large groups I liked to address them initially with a few positive comments and perhaps some general procedural or policy statements. Following this brief introduction I would break the group into smaller units, depending on how many supervisors I had. Learning in a small group environment is much faster and more focused. It allows for much better discussion and give and take. It also reinforces the idea that you expect your supervisors to know their job duties as well as you do.

Written tests are a good way to help your staff focus on the material that you present. While I almost never actually graded the exams, the fact that a test awaits at the end of the training always serves as good motivation to maintain interest throughout the training. By handing out the exam at the beginning of the training the employees could better focus on the critical subject matter as it was introduced. It is also valuable to go over each test answer and field questions at the conclusion of the training. Train your supervisors to listen to your line employees and don't be afraid to draw on their experiences. While you and your supervisors may be the experts on your particular operation, many of your line employees will bring greater experience in specific areas of expertise.

Training has the following benefits:

- Improved service levels
- Improved productivity
- Reduced product and equipment cost
- Better morale
- Lower turnover

Holding quarterly employee meetings or one-day on-the-job training sessions just won't get it done! Every workday should be looked at as an opportunity to develop your staff. The better you train and motivate your staff, the better they will perform and the easier your job will become.

4. Document Procedures

The first step in establishing and maintaining a quality training program is to have written policies and procedures. While most banquet operations have service standards and policies, few take the necessary time and effort to completely document the many details in a concise, understandable format. If you are not comfortable with the assignment, then delegate and edit. But get it down in black and white!

Similar to my experiences with short-staffing, good documentation is another area where many catering operations fail to apply the proper energy. Clearly, producing technical documents that are clear and concise is not something that everyone can do. But every manager is capable of at least jotting down the steps involved in their procedures. From such a list, any writer with a decent word processor can put together a workable manual.

My approach to documentation is to simplify and reduce. I find documentation to be the most effective when it is broken down by position. Chronologically listing the steps involved in each of the position's job duties. I have included some sample documentation for a banquet captain in addendum.

Documenting your procedures is helpful in the following ways:

- Maintaining consistency of standards over time
- Training of new employees
- Holding employees accountable for their performance

Without documentation it is very difficult to hold your employees to consistent standards. In a business with as many changing variables as catering, it is critical to establish guidelines for those variables that do not change.

5. Create An Employee Database

Just as you use a client database to help you manage the sales function, an employee database will help you in booking, scheduling and maintaining accurate records of employee attendance and performance. It is also a convenient way to pull up current names and phone numbers (by position if you want), when booking for upcoming events. Scheduling is not an art, but a science. Confirm by initials or code every booked employee or cancellation. Establish a methodology and stick to it. Nothing is more frustrating than miscommunication on scheduling. Employees do not mind policies and rules as long as they are clearly communicated and applied consistently.

The database can also make extrapolations of costs a much easier process. Simply highlight the employees who worked a particular function, input their hours, and have the computer spit out the reports.

6. Focus on Employee Morale

Another shortcoming that I have encountered on a consistent basis is poor morale. Achieving truly high morale among your entire staff requires great commitment. It takes years of experience and extraordinary personal qualities. Yet it is something every manager should strive for. The days of expecting employees to be grateful just to have a job are long gone. Since we have established that we need our employees more than they need us, it makes sense to act like it. Let me focus on a few simple behavioral characteristics that any person in a supervisory role should adopt.

- Follow the golden rule. Treat your employees the way you would like to be treated. This is so obvious that it should go without saying.

- Praise your employees at every opportunity. Sincerely thank your employees for completing even the smallest of tasks. This should become a habit. This simple idea is more valuable in a manager than any amount of technical knowledge. I would prefer a supervisor who understood this concept to a Cornell graduate who did not, in every case, for any type of operation.

- Pass along as much information to your employees as you can. Everything that you know (that is not confidential) should be made available to your staff. This makes them feel more a part of the firm and not just a low-level worker.

- Focus on training as a daily function of everyone's job. I made it a point to conduct formal and informal training meetings whenever we had spare moments between functions. The more everyone knows, the easier everyone's job becomes.

- Treat everyone fairly. This can be quite tricky when you are trying to maintain high productivity, reward achievement, and address performance shortfalls. I have found that a strict reliance on your written policies and procedures is the one failsafe way to approach this challenge. As long as everyone knows what is expected on them, then it is a relatively easy matter to mete out praise and counsel based on your documented policies and procedures.

- Do not hesitate to address behavioral or attitude problems. These types of behaviors will affect everyone negatively. I don't care how long an employee has worked at the firm, or how good they are at their job, if an employee displays negative attitudes about management, the firm's policies, or other employees, they are a net negative to the organization. By following the steps I discuss in the section on counseling you will be able to resolve this matter one way or the other. Tolerating these types of behaviors will prevent you from creating a truly high-performing, enjoyable workplace.

7. Counseling

Counseling employees is an unpleasant but necessary part of meeting your productivity and morale goals. It is perhaps the most difficult task that a manager must brave, but it is a requirement of the job, and should never be put off simply because it is uncomfortable. Like most seasoned food service managers I have counseled, disciplined, written-up and fired numerous employees.

To me, there are really several different levels of counseling. One form of counseling is more casual and may be directed either to an individual or the entire group. This type of counseling takes the form of a gentle reminder. Such comments as: "Be sure you don't forget to clean the stockroom tonight, OK Tony?" Or you may, when addressing the entire group, remind everyone that we did not do as good a job in pre-bussing during the last dinner as we would have liked. The key to passing along these types of comments is to keep them to a minimum, and to smile when you speak. Be sure that you're employees know that these are friendly reminders and not intended to be warnings or threats. As long as you recognize your employees, both individually and as a group, when they do meet your expectations, occasional informal reminders will not be processed negatively.

The other type of counseling is conducted when an employee has violated a specific policy, or has shown a pattern of behavior which, in their sum, amount to a violation of some more general policy, such as insubordination, or disregard for company property. Unless it is clear that the employee has committed an offense warranting termination, the objective of any counseling session should be to make the employee a more productive, valuable employee. Until you have given them their last paycheck your interests are best served by helping the employee to improve on their areas of weakness. In the formal counseling session your employee handbook is your source of guidance. In order to be fair and legal, you must adhere to the letter and the intent of your written policies. When dealing with formal counseling, whether oral or written, you must be consistent with all employees in your enforcement of the company's policies. Failure to do so can cause significant morale problems and possibly lawsuits. By following the company's policies regarding counseling and reprimands you will protect yourself, your department and your firm. That being said, here are a few specific recommendations on how to approach this difficult task.

1. Find a place that is private and be sure to allow enough time to complete the counseling session without interruptions.

2. Be sure you have your facts straight. If there are eyewitnesses to the behavior be sure that all stories are accounted for and there are no lose ends in your reports.

3. If there are documents or physical evidence involved be sure that you bring the documents or some specific record of the physical evidence with you to the counseling session.

4. Be sure you have reviewed the employee's file before you schedule the counseling session. Depending on the offense, and their previously documented reprimands, the employee may be subject to suspension and/or termination. Follow your firm's policies to the letter on these determinations and consult with human resources as warranted.

5. Address the matter directly and quickly, stating all the facts that you have at hand. At this point it is good to pause and see if the employee is going to dispute your charges, attempt to explain the behavior, or accept your analysis.

6. If you are confident in your facts, and the employee insists on disputing them, it is advisable to end that part of the discussion with a simple phrase, "You obviously disagree with me on these facts, and if you feel strongly about it you are welcome to pursue this matter with my boss. For the purposes of this discussion we are going to move on."

7. Explain why their behavior is a problem for the organization, but do not personalize your counseling. Instead, focus on the employee's behavior and the firm's policies. Your role should be as an administrator, not a judge. This is where you should attempt to get the employee to understand why their behavior is unacceptable to the firm and to help them develop a corrective plan of action.

8. Move swiftly to the consequences of their action. "I have documented what I have just explained to you. There is a place here for your signature that documents that I discussed this matter with you. One copy is for your records, one copy will go in your file in the personnel office and I'll keep a copy here in my office. Once again, if you would prefer to discuss this further, I will be glad to arrange a meeting with my boss and/or a representative or human resources."

9. Normally, it is a good conclusion to state your perceptions of the employees better qualities and make it clear that your interest is in keeping this employee a productive, valuable employee on your staff. It may also makes sense to state what the consequences are of their inability to correct their behavior, that it may lead to more formal counseling and possibly termination. These are the policies. By discussing the matter in such specific terms there will be no surprises if the employee persists in the negative behavior.

Chapter 3

Managing the Kitchen

Invariably, it will be the quality of your food that will distinguish your operation from the competition. Think of your own conversations with your friends and associates when you discuss your latest adventures in a restaurant. The quality of the food almost always takes precedence. No amount of clever, polished service can make up for lousy food. All the pieces of your catering puzzle must come together to pull off a top-notch banquet, but it will never get off the ground without a quality kitchen operation. We could include hundreds of recipes, menus and themed buffets in this text, but this is not a recipe book. There are more than enough of those around. Instead, let us focus on what it takes to put together a quality kitchen operation and keep it performing at a high level.

1. Staffing and Training

A quality kitchen operation, like the rest of your operation, requires competent and motivated employees in order to run properly. Chefs, kitchen managers and cooks are skilled employees and they are in high demand. This doesn't mean, however, that you must always pay top dollar to attract the finest talent. By establishing and maintaining a professional environment where consistency in management systems are practiced and creativity is encouraged, you will find that great chefs are easier to attract and good chefs can be developed into great ones. If cooking is not your forte, then spend whatever time is needed to learn at least the basics of the craft. Chefs can be notoriously friendly, (when approached with a dash of humility and a dollop of courtesy). Every manager should spend time in the thick of the food preparation process. This provides much needed insight into the demands of the job. In addition, you never know when you will be needed to fill-in when production is behind schedule. You should be fully prepared for such an eventuality. As with all management positions, your chefs should be accountable for developing their subordinates and rewarded when their efforts show results.

2. Listen To Your Chef

You're top culinary employees----whether executive chefs, kitchen managers, or simply experienced cooks----should be included in the sales and planning process. Your chefs know the most about your principal product, your food, and they are invaluable when you need to guide the client toward menu items that can be prepared tastily *and* profitably. Salespeople should never sell any item that is not on the menu without first running it by the chef. It is not only risky, but it shows a lack of respect for the culinary management group.

Involve your kitchen staff in all aspects of the planning process. The culinary staff should be consulted on all large events, VIP clients and service planning meetings. Not only are their suggestions extremely helpful, but involving the kitchen staff in all discussions goes along way towards developing a cohesive team.

3. Keep Your Kitchen Organized

You can never be too organized. The first step in controlling costs (both food and labor) is to organize the storage of your foods, beverages and equipment. Even more important is kitchen sanitation; it is a reflection of your attitude toward your product. At best a dirty kitchen creates a negative image and poor morale. At its worse, it can lead to health hazards, diminishment of your reputation, loss of your business and legal problems. Like staffing, cleaning is an hourly, daily, continuous task. Along those lines, here are a few concepts that should be adopted:

- Organize your food stock in logical, easy-to-rotate locations.
- Put those items you use the most, closest to the prep areas.
- Establish a cleaning checklist with dates, times and assigned personnel.
- Label/date all prepped food and rotate religiously.

- Freeze and re-use food whenever possible, if only for employee meals.

- Regularly hold training meetings on food service sanitation.

- Recognize and reward employees who show initiative in improving the cleanliness and appearance of your operation.

- Post food safety awareness posters in appropriate locations.

4. The Dangers of Cross-Contamination

Accidental food-to-food or surface-to-surface cross-contamination is one of the biggest culprits of food-borne illness. Consider this example: Suppose you spill some raw poultry juice on the prep table while preparing a chicken dish. You then wipe up the juice with a cloth and proceed to cut lettuce on the same contaminated surface. Although the counter may look clean, bacteria from the poultry may still be present---- and may have transferred to the lettuce. When the lettuce is used to prepare a salad you now run the risk of spreading a food-borne illness.

Your hands can also help spread food-borne bacteria to less obvious places: the refrigerator, door handles, hot and cold sink faucets, dishcloths, and counter-tops. It is paramount to wash your hands thoroughly after handling any food items directly. You should also clean and sanitize all prep surfaces frequently with an antibacterial agent.

You should organize the storage of your refrigerated foods wisely, paying close attention to the potential for cross-product contamination. Never store poultry or beef above one another. Always be sure that product that goes into the cooler is in a lidded container and is properly labeled and dated.

5. Common Bacterial Dangers

Following are the four main microscopic organisms that are spread through improper food handling and cross-contamination.

Salmonella:

Lives in the intestinal tracts of humans and animals. Often found in raw or undercooked foods, such as poultry, eggs and meat. Can also be found in un-pasteurized milk. Improper hand washing procedures can spread these bacteria. Can also be spread through cross-contamination between poultry and meat products.

Escherichia Coli 0157: (E. coli):

Most often found in raw or rare ground beef. E. Coli has also been associated with outbreaks involving fresh produce and apple cider. Improper hand washing procedures can spread these bacteria.

Staphylococcus Aureus (Staph):

Staph bacteria are found on our skin, in infected cuts and pimples, and in our noses and throats. Staph can multiply rapidly at warm temperatures to produce a toxin that causes illness. Staph bacteria prefer cooked food high in protein. They also grow in foods high in sugar or salt. All employees should wear proper bandages and gloves when handling food.

Campylobacter Jejuni:

This may be present in raw or undercooked meat, poultry or shellfish. Other sources include un-pasteurized milk, untreated drinking water and rodents.

Remember that bacteria need two things in order to grow----food and the right temperature. Because bacteria grow so quickly (through asexual reproduction) they can multiply from a few hundred to a few million very quickly. The optimum temperature for bacteria (what is called the danger zone) is from 32 to 212 Fahrenheit. This is why certain foods (particularly meats) are normally prepared at high temperatures. This is also why it is critical to return product to cold storage as soon as practical.

As bacteria multiply in a food product they create toxins that will not normally be eliminated by cooking, regardless of how high the temperature is. This is why once a food product is spoiled, cooking to high temperatures does not remove the threat of poisoning. It is a good idea to conduct food safety classes with your kitchen staff on a regular basis. A single food-borne illness can cost you your business.

6. Contamination Dangers

Another common danger that all food service professionals should be aware of is the danger of non-biological contaminants. These include such things as chemicals, hair, dirt, glass, metal, wood, cardboard and paper. In the many steps involved in transporting, storing, preparing and delivering foods it is quite easy to accidentally contaminate your product with any number of contaminants. The following guidelines will help to reduce your exposure to this danger.

- Follow the four-step method when cleaning utensils: wash, rinse, sanitize and rinse.

- Be sure your dishwashers are working to specification. Heat is your best enemy against bacteria. You must also be sure that the rinse cycle is properly removing any detergent.

- When using cleansers on walls and prep surfaces be sure to follow with a water rinse and a dry cloth.

- Whenever possible store product in clear, plastic containers with lids. Storing product in cardboard boxes or wood crates increases the potential for contamination.

- Demand that all kitchen employees wear gloves and appropriate hats.

7. Keeping Out Pests

One of the most expensive, frustrating and embarrassing problems that a caterer can confront is the problem of pest infestation in the workplace. Once infested, an establishment must devote serious financial resources, effort and time to eliminate the infestation. Few things will harm your reputation more than the sight of pests on your premises. Most professionals who have worked in this business for any length of time have worked somewhere where bugs or rodents were a problem. There is nothing worse than a roach crawling across your floor during an event, or, God forbid, across a dinner table. Your goal must be to prevent infestation before it occurs.

Practicing the fundamentals of sanitation should be, of course, your first and best strategy when it comes to controlling the threat of pests. All pests need food to survive, breed and nest. If you remove their food sources you don't present a very hospitable environment. Maintaining a rigorous schedule of treatment with an exterminator is also a necessity. Once again, trying to remove pests once they are established is many times more expensive than controlling them before they have made a home.

Be aware of possible sources of entry into your establishment: open doors or windows, cracks in walls and in boxes delivered by vendors. Management should inspect in detail all the areas of their property on a weekly basis. You should be on the lookout for signs of infestation, such things as rat droppings, gnawed food or boxes, and roach specs. Wherever you encounter pests be sure your staff takes them seriously. Failure to do so can ultimately close down your business.

8. Food Purchasing

Clearly, one of the most difficult tasks confronting your kitchen management staff is the accurate, quality-conscious, and cost-efficient ordering of food. Like all catering tasks, however, there are a few basic systems one can follow that will make the purchasing of food a manageable process.

- Design your inventory forms so they match the physical locations of your stock. (Of course this implies that your stock is organized logically). This simple idea will greatly speed up the inventory process.

- Include your inventory unit, units per case, pack/size, par and vendor code on your inventory forms.

- Establish pars for staple items that are always kept on hand. Inventory and re-order weekly at a minimum.

- Explode your menu to all its ingredients, with the precise quantities that are needed, and put together a few sample runs of quantities needed for different guest counts.

- Develop a menu explosion form that lists your menu items, along with the quantities of side items that are sold with each item.

- When an event is sold, use your explosion forms to project the total quantity needed of each menu item, then simply deduct the quantities on hand to compute your order.

- Establish a vendor database and establish guidelines that require several quotes before making a major purchase.

- Have your vendors supply you with order forms. (Have them customize them if they really want your business.)

- Integrate your inventory forms with your vendor database to automate the ordering process.

- Fax your orders whenever possible. (This provides both parties with a hard copy and saves valuable time on the phone).

- Be nice to your vendors. Even though you are the customer, there will always come a time when you'll have to ask them for efforts beyond the scope of their normal duties.

- Establish rigid rules for checking in deliveries. Few operations would trust this duty to anyone not in management. Be certain that every detail of your purchase order matches the invoice *and* the actual products delivered. Mistakes will happen every day with deliveries. You should always reconcile the purchase order with the invoice and the actual product received.

- Keep your product stored in a logical, organized, easy-to-access and inventory manner. (We already covered this, but it needs to be mentioned twice).

9. Controlling Food Costs

Your food product is the largest single expense of your catering operation. Your ability to manage food cost can be the difference between making a profit and losing your shirt. The best kitchens ingrain the awareness of food cost into every employee. Not a single sprig of parsley should be brushed away into the trashcan without a tear. Your kitchen operation must start and end with one overriding premise: zero tolerance for waste!

Your ability to organize, inventory and order stock will play a big part in your ability to control waste, but other kitchen management concepts will be needed to meet your cost objectives. Listed below are a few traditional ideas that are widely used to keep the food preparation process cost-efficient.

- Train, train, train! Every shift should be viewed as an opportunity to pass on some of your expertise in food preparation. In short order you will find that not only are your cooks more efficient, but the food looks and tastes better as well. If you do not develop your kitchen staff, your operation will be doomed to mediocrity.

- Establish a daily inventory system for your meats and seafood that reconciles items sold with actual usage.

- Keep your coolers and storage areas locked when not is use. (Employee theft is often the largest single cause of high food cost.)

- Label and date everything that you purchase or prep, and establish strict guidelines on product rotation.

- Keep plenty of clean, accurate scales on hand, as well as measuring cups and spoons, and be sure they are used.

- Purchase clear, plastic holding containers that are stackable for the storage of prepped product.

- Put your recipes on laminated recipe cards and require their use by all employees.

- Recognize a kitchen employee as a food cost captain each month to assist in administrative duties related to food cost controls.

- Keep a close eye on the temperature of your coolers and freezers. A jump of just a few degrees can make a big difference in the shelf life of perishables.

- Funnel all excess prepped or perishable inventory to the employee cafeteria.

- Communicate any overages in product to the sales staff.

- Maintain a focus on quality and presentation over quantity.

- Establish incentive programs for your chefs and kitchen staff for meeting budgeted food cost.

- Post the purchase prices of your food items as a reminder to control waste.

10. Preparation, Cooking, and Dishing Out

For the kitchen, functions flow (from a time perspective), in reverse. Doors opening time is zero hour. The chef must use his/her experience to plan the preparation, cooking and dishing out of each item so that everything is as fresh as possible, served at the right temperatures, set in the right place, and all at just the right time. If it takes an hour and a half to cook the roast, an hour to slice it, another thirty minutes to dish it out, and another thirty minutes to move it to the room, then you'd better be sure you have some meat burning two and a half hours prior to serve out. These are the types of formulas that banquet chefs must work with daily.

And it's not always so straightforward. Often, there are numerous functions taking place at the same time. It is not uncommon in the hotel business to have every meeting room, conference center and ballroom hosting some sort of function, at the same time----and perhaps some hospitality suites as well. (You have to love your salespeople on such a night.) Getting everything prepared on time and shipped to the right location is a big job; you'd better have a plan. All the knowledge needed to cook and dish out for large groups is two or three books in itself. You'd better hope your chef has the experience to put it together. But let us list at least a few ideas and administrative concepts which many firms have found useful in managing the timing and product flow of prepared food in a banquet setting.

- Plan your prep activities before completing your employee schedules.

- Work *at least* a day ahead as much as possible.

- Always be sure your plates are pulled at least a day ahead.

- Once plates are pulled, the set count should be set aside, secured and labeled.

- Clearly label and date any product in cooler storage. Attach a copy of the BEO.

- Use ice baths on cold vegetables where appropriate.

- Turn your hot boxes on at least an hour prior to dish out and be sure to check the temperatures.

- During large dish-outs make an all-call to any available staff (including administrative or sales personnel if available), to speed up the process.

- The Top Dog in the kitchen should always be at the end of the dish out assembly line.

- Be sure you have someone who can count putting the plates into the hot boxes or cold racks.

- Figure in the time that a product will remain in the hot box before serving, and back out your cooking time accordingly. This is a touchy and challenging concept, but it can make the difference between an excellent meal and a poor one.

- Do not overload carts, rolling racks and hot boxes.

- Allow no cart or hotbox to leave the kitchen without attaching a copy of the BEO.

- Be sure to inventory the items on each cart or hotbox as they leave the kitchen as one last check to be sure all the counts match.

- Never allow any finished product to exit the kitchen without the proper escort.

Chapter 4

Setting the Room

For many, it is the design and set-up of the dining area that provides the greatest impact to the guests and the biggest sense of creative expression to the caterer. Indeed, setting an elegant room can make an impression that can last for many banquets to come. But setting a room properly, particularly when the size of the party gets much beyond a couple hundred, can also be more challenging than one may first suspect. Putting together a dining area which makes the best possible impact, while keeping the room serviceable, and more importantly, not wasting all your profit margin on set-up, is a task that requires good planning and years of experience.

Buffets

Buffet design and set-up can be one of the most creative and impressive aspects of catering. It can also be costly, time-consuming and confusing. We will discuss several techniques for managing the buffet set-up process. Remember that within any plan, your food should always remain the primary focus.

1. Using Diagrams

Almost all banquet operations make use of diagrams when mapping out a room set-up. Diagrams are extremely useful tools when communicating your plans to your clients and your service staff. Many operations have drawings of their most common table sets (with numbers or labels), to speed up the planning process. There is plenty of software available to make the diagramming process fast, fun and efficient. Once the actual table drops are finalized, one can arrow in the exact locations to place the food. Remember that the table design flows from what is on the menu, and the table location flows from the room in which they are set, the number of guests, the timing of their arrival and departure, and the actual inventory of table shapes available. It is wise to know exactly how many of each type of table is available for a specific function.

Never lose sight of functionality (FLOW!). Always walk the table set in your mind as though you were the guest. Be sure everything flows logically and naturally.

2. Creative Elements

Once you have determined the table locations, their shapes, and some sense of where the food will be placed, you will use your creative ability to create a stage on which to feature your food. Listed below are some of the most common techniques in bringing to fruition creative designs.

- Remember that your food should always be the principal focus of your guests' attention.

- Pay close attention to the blending of colors and lighting.

- Purchase decor fabrics that match your tablecloths, napkins and skirting. You may have several groups of fabrics (flowered, black and white themes, picnic style, southwestern----you get the idea).

- Assign specific buffets to your captains or wait staff from set-up, through service and breakdown. This gives a focus of responsibility and accountability, as well as a sense of ownership and pride in their work.

- Use glass racks, boxes, cans, kitchen pans (or anything for that matter), to create risers and terraces.

- Cover your risers with tablecloths, either in a ruffled, flowery effect, or with the folds wrapped around tightly in a layered effect.

- Purchase bright fabrics such as lame for featured items such as desserts or cold seafood.

- Plan your use of florals with care. A small, elegant floral can often be more effective than a large bush full of geraniums.

Whatever you finally decide on, don't order a single carnation until you determine your table sets. Floral placement flows from table drops and food placement.

- Use greenery of all sorts to fill dead spots, after everything else has been placed. Old florals provide a ready resource for fill-in greenery.

- Keep a storeroom full of props. Such items as vases and urns, various size baskets, mirrors, roman columns, Mexican hats and other theme items create excellent and inexpensive backdrops.

- Almost anything can be a prop. Always be on the lookout for new ideas. Listen to the suggestions of your staff.

- Many items, such as cheese, bread, chips, crackers and vegetables, can be displayed in open presentations, as though pouring out of a basket or bowl, or simply a ruffled tablecloth.

- Use kitchen items such as raw pasta, cooking oils, sauces, etc. as props for chef's stations.

- Involve the kitchen staff in buffet set-up and serve out.

- Feature chef's stations whenever your budget allows. With large parties be sure to have generous portions pre-prepared, ready to serve.

- Always consider the option of passing some or all of your cold hors d'ouevres. This makes for an added touch of elegance and may free up space on your buffets.

- Use small and large candles strategically placed for elegant accents.

- When serving china it is a good idea to place your bus trays and tray jacks beside your trashcans.

Seated Functions

The set-up of seated functions, just like buffets, begins with the actual table locations. This would seem to be a fairly routine task. However, there are numerous variables that can make the job difficult. For example: Set counts sometimes are not finalized until just before the meal is served; or perhaps you must take into account audio/visual equipment set in the middle of the room; or VIP and head tables that must be in a certain location and only set for a specified number; or perhaps you're feeding the crew in a back hallway or dressing room and these meals are part of your count. All these considerations (and many more) make it imperative to start with and maintain an accurate diagram.

Your table assignments for the service staff will also flow from the diagram. Obviously, if there are mistakes on the diagram there will be confusion in the dining room. The process of communicating changes from the client to the sales associates, then to the operations staff, and finally to the set-up staff, is prone to errors. Any banquet supervisor worth his/her salt will personally count the tables to be sure they match the agreed-upon set, as well as ensure that the table locations match their diagram.

The spacing between tables and aisles will flow----there's that word again----from the set count and the room. Most operations start with a standard 10-foot center (from the middle of one table to the middle of the next), and at least 10-foot aisles. A 9-foot center is about as close as you can get and still serve a meal. Eleven or 12-foot centers will sometimes make your guests feel isolated from the other guests at the banquet, but they are useful when employing more elaborate service styles. Make it a rule, not a guideline to measure every table that is dropped. Eyeballing it can get you into a mess with large sets, and eventually you may have to start over.

Chair placement is also important to a properly set dining room. With a 10-top, you should place one chair at 12 o'clock (toward the head table) and one at six. The other four chairs on each side should be equally spaced. With an 8-top, chairs are aligned at twelve, six, three and nine, with the remaining four in the open spaces. All eight chairs should be directly aligned with the chair opposite. With nine or 11-counts, you'll have to pick a consistent starting point (12 o'clock say), and work out the spacing as best you can. Many managers never realize that the first step to setting a table is to have the chairs arranged properly. Because your place settings are aligned with your chairs, if your chairs are sloppily dropped then your table will appear sloppy (i.e. not evenly spaced). You should never allow your staff to place a single fork until the chairs are properly set.

Similarly, your tablecloths should always be dropped right-side up, with the center seam running straight towards the front of the room, or the head table. The corners of the tablecloth should be tucked in and should not rest on any of the chair seats.

2. Standard Sets

At some point you will find it useful to determine what your standard table sets will be for breakfast, lunch, dinner and VIP functions. While the number of forks and spoons will flow from the menu, you will still need to determine how many knives, creamers, butters, dressings, etc. you will need to place; and where you will place them. For example: Is the ice water placed over the teaspoon? How far from the table edge is the coffee cup? How is the coffee cup handle placed? Where do you set the sugar bowl(s)? How many sugar packets should be served in the bowl? All these questions should be answered and documented. Without standards, it is extremely difficult to train your staff and hold them accountable.

3. Equipment Pulls

One of the first steps in putting together a seated function is computing and pulling what equipment you will need to set the room. It is wise to have a form designed that lists every piece of equipment in your inventory, along with room for miscellaneous items and notes. The process of working your way through such a form will make it more difficult to miss an item you will need. If you work in outside catering, forgetting even a single fork is unacceptable.

The quantity of each item needed will flow from three considerations: the menu, the set count and your established standards. Your standards should not change from day to day, the menu should be finalized well before you pull your equipment, and you should have a pretty firm guess on the set count at least a day out.

Once the equipment has been pulled, often by the stewarding department, it should be checked by a banquet captain or supervisor prior to beginning the set. Any equipment shortages can then be communicated to the stewarding department to complete the pull. If you are an outside catering operation, then there are no second chances. Your pull must be computed accurately from the start and checked before leaving the premises. It is often useful to have a different person checking the pull from the one who computed the pull form. Whether you run an in-house operation or an outside catering firm, equipment shortages waste valuable time (which costs you money in labor), and may even result in the room not being set before the doors open. If you cannot manage the process of completing a pull sheet and getting the equipment to the room, you will always be in a scramble to complete the room set. Teach your staff how to add and subtract and push for perfection.

Once you have managed to get the right quantities of equipment to the room and the equipment has been checked for accuracy, there is only one more step before you can begin the room set: staging. It will save you valuable time and confusion if you assign a captain or two to separate and sort the equipment to make it easy to find and access. With larger sets you may want to drop a few extra eight foots in the aisle on which to place the silverware. Another idea (one that is particularly useful with sets over 1,000) is to place the silverware on carts that can be rolled into the dining room as the set progresses. Some banquet managers will stage serving ware at various locations throughout the room, or at both ends, to save time and labor walking back and forth. In addition to staging the equipment, you should not forget to have plenty of wiping cloths and hot water on hand when the waiters arrive.

While these ideas many seem picayune to some, I can't begin to tell you how many times I've seen a room full of waiters standing around burning up clock-time (and labor cost) waiting for wiping cloths or water, or searching for equipment. The best banquet managers are always thinking 30 minutes to an hour ahead of what is happening now. The objective is to keep your service staff productive by providing them with everything they need as close as you can to where and when they need it.

4. Organizing the Staff and Setting the Room

While it may seem (at first glance) a little far-fetched, it is possible to set a dining room for 10,000 guests, quietly and efficiently, without misplacing a single item at a single table. But you must have a plan, and your staff must be able to understand it and follow it through. There are many approaches to setting a dining room, and each approach has certain advantages; and disadvantages.

Before we introduce the most common methods, let me mention one idea shared by all of them: the sample table. A senior captain should always be assigned to set one table completely, to serve as an example of what all the other tables should look like. If the banquet management staff does nothing else during the rest of the set, they should definitely review the sample table for accuracy. Your objective should be to have an entire dining room identical to the sample table.

Another idea (which I certainly recommend) is to have each waiter sign in with his or her captain when first arriving on the floor. Throughout the entire banquet you should keep your wait staff alongside their captains. This establishes a team concept and also maintains accountability and a chain of command. By communicating with your captains you can pass along information to every member of your staff. Captains also should give their waiters their table assignments as they come on to the floor. If you give them their assignments in writing (on a small note for example), it will prevent you from having to remind them repeatedly throughout the function. (I've seen waiters forget what tables they were assigned halfway into the function!) This also allows them the opportunity to become familiar with where their tables are located during the room set.

Set Your Own Tables Method

This method is by far the simplest approach to setting a dining room, and for small functions it works very well. Simply assign waiters their tables as they clock in, direct them to the sample table, and let them have at it. When setting a room of less than about 30 rounds this method usually works fine.

Advantages

- Gives wait staff a narrow area of focus.

- Establishes ownership and a sense of pride in one's assigned area.

- Requires a minimum of instruction to get the waiters started.

- Waiters become totally familiar with their table locations in the room.

Disadvantages

- If some of your staff is late arriving, some tables may be late being set.

- Your faster waiters may finish quickly and disappear, or feel slighted when they are asked to assist other, slower waiters.

- Your faster waiters may tend to slow down their pace to match everyone else.

- Equipment may get spread out across the room, causing confusion by those staff members who can't locate the equipment they need.

- It is difficult for the room supervisor to have a solid feel on how well the set is progressing.

- It is difficult for the captains to oversee the quality of each table.

- Dropping ice water and pre-set salads and desserts may be disorganized.

Captains Set Their Own Section Method

This method is used by many operations because it seems to offer some of the benefits of the Set Your Own Tables Method, while allowing the room captains freedom to utilize their staff in any way needed to maximize productivity.

Advantages

- The set can proceed in a timely fashion despite late arrivals.

- Promotes a sense of teamwork within the captain's group, which makes it easier to utilize your more experienced staff to help others.

- Does not spread out equipment nearly as much as when each waiter grabs his own stock.

- Provides a good chain of communication when trying to locate equipment.

- Gives the captains a sense of ownership and pride in their section.

Disadvantages

- Equipment will still tend to get spread out to the various sections. (Some captains will even hoard it to get ahead).

- Less effective captains will tend to be slower and sloppier with their set.

Pre-stage On Ovals Method

The idea behind this method is to pre-stage the equipment for each table on an oval tray before the wait staff arrives. Thus, all the waiters have to do is grab an oval for each of his/her tables and begin setting. The silverware may even be polished ahead of time if there are time and labor restraints. Most often, this method is used when there is a quick room turn, or other time constraints.

Advantages

- Pre-sorts all the equipment for each table, hopefully eliminating in-the-room shortages.

- Reduces hourly labor for service staff.

- Speeds up room-set significantly.

- Usually your best option for setting a room when there is an extremely quick turn.

Disadvantages

- Someone has to be paid to pre-sort and polish the equipment. Unless you have hourly employees making less than your wait staff, then you end up with a net loss.

- It is impossible to check the quantity and quality of the pre-sort. If the duty is done by your least paid workers you are likely to get sub-par work.

- Almost all waiters will tend to re-polish silver before it is placed on a table (just by reflex), thus negating the advantages of pre-polishing.

- You will not know if there are equipment shortages at particular tables until you are well into the set.

The Wave Method

The Wave Method involves a few more steps than any of the previous methods, but it is extremely effective if managed properly, particularly when faced with the task of setting very large rooms. Several procedures must come together to make The Wave Method work properly, but when the plan works you will be surprised at how easily a large room can come together, on time, with a great consistency of standards.

The first step in this method is to give your captains specific set-up assignments, not by location, but by equipment. One captain might be responsible for forks and B&B's for example, while another does knives and coffee cups. Still another might drop only centerpieces, candles, sugar bowls and salt and pepper (in fact, it works best if one or more captains are assigned solely to centers). Their job is to drop their assigned items throughout the entire dining room.

All staff should start at one side of the room and progress to the other, being sure to finish each aisle before moving to the next. Thus you have an entire group of wait staff focused on doing nothing but dropping forks, from one end of the room to the other; and when that is finished, they begin on B&B's, and so forth. Everyone will work together to drop any pre-sets, including ice water. In the addendum is an example form for making Wave Set assignments. This method may seem, on first inspection, to be fraught with problems, but allow me to analyze it more closely.

Advantages

- Equipment is isolated only with the group that is dropping it, virtually eliminating any time wasted searching for equipment in the dining room.

- Equipment can be rolled across the room along with the group that is setting it, speeding up the time spent walking back and forth for another handful.

- Waiters are focused on only one task at a time. It was proven long ago that repetition tends to improve productivity and quality.

- Captains are focused on only a few tasks, providing for better accountability and performance.

- There is a clear chain of command when a table is missing something.

- It is easier to get a feel for how well the set is progressing since it moves logically across the room.

- Any equipment shortages will be isolated along the same area (generally the last aisle).

- It is easier to roll staff from one group to another if needed.

- Late arriving staff can be integrated into the set easily.

- The process of dropping centers is greatly improved if only a few are handling and setting these items (florals, creamers, butter, sugar, s&p, etc.).

- All leftover equipment will tend to end up at one location (the far end of the room), making it easier for stewarding to recover.

- Dropping pre-sets and water is easier because your waiters are in a pattern of dropping from one side to the other already.

Disadvantages

- Assignments must be done carefully and logically (see addendum) for it to work properly.

- Waiters may lose a sense of ownership in their stations since they do not set their own tables.

- An ineffective captain may leave his/her mark on the entire room rather than just a few tables.

- Waiters are not directly exposed to their table assignments during the room set.

Methods 101: In Conclusion

As you can see, each of these methods has its own pluses and minuses; and in certain situations, for certain events, they all work fine. Often, time constraints and other variables require you to create entirely new approaches. That's part of the fun! Almost any plan, ultimately, will succeed, as long as you allow enough time and clearly communicate your plan to the staff.

5. How Long Should A Room Set Take?

If you are staffing at 1 waiter per 3 tables the following formulas work pretty well.

Number of Guests	Time
1 - 300	2 hours
300 - 1500	2.5 hours
1500 - 3000	3 hours
3000 - 5000	3.5 hours
over 5000	4 hours or more

On sets over 1000 it is usually a good idea to complete some of the set-up tasks early, preferably on the day prior. Such tasks would include dropping tablecloths and centers, folding napkins, staging equipment, and completing all planning meetings and administrative tasks.

6. A Word about Managing the Set

Many of the ideas and strategies that are presented in this book are geared toward higher-volume operations. When dealing with small sets (under 100, say), applying elaborate set-up strategies is a waste of time. It is only when you get to the larger numbers that equipment and time issues become important. When you are staring down 700 rounds, you'd better have a plan! Setting a dining room properly is an art. Some banquet managers catch on to it pretty quickly, while others will struggle with it throughout their careers.

Too often we witness the phenomenon of banquet managers who attempt to produce results through intimidation and threatening behavior. Some even resort to yelling across the room in an attempt to motivate and speed up the room-set process. Such behavior is self-defeating. Humans are social creatures, and will tend to form a connection to whatever group activity they are involved in. If you encourage teamwork and reward achievement, your staff will respond with positive results. Communicating with your staff in any style that demeans or insults them will result in their disassociation from your goals and (with some), a desire to see your efforts fail.

Catering is a business, not a leisure activity. But it is a business filled with people. If your staff is not happy, or positively motivated (for the right reasons), it will show up every time in poor service levels and turnover. Plan your sets wisely, communicate your plan to the team clearly, speak to every employee professionally, and praise achievement at every opportunity.

8. Back Aisle Staging and Organization

Just as you plan the flow of your guest service in the dining room, you should also plan the flow of the back aisle where your service staff will pick up food and beverages and drop off any dishes from the room. The organization of your back aisle can make or break even the smallest of functions; I've seen it a thousand times. Basically there are three separate stations in a back-aisle set-up: dish-out, breakdown and beverage.

Your dish-out is the area where your hot and cold boxes are located, and where your stewards or kitchen staff will assist in dishing out the prepared food during the function. Most operations place ovals on top of the hot boxes and 8-foot tables in front to speed up the dish-out process. Waiters will queue up and then call for the number of plates they need on the next oval. For large, spread-out receptions, you will need to organize the food boxes so the proper back-up product can be rolled to the proper staging area.

Breakdown stations usually consist of a series of tables (often double-stacked), with empty dish dollies, glass racks, bus tubs and trash cans set behind them. Be sure to keep some extra cleaning towels, as well as a broom and mop. Allowing your back aisle to remain wet or soiled can cause injuries.

The beverage station must be in an easy-to-access location and it must be logically set up with the proper quantities of equipment, ice and beverages. Back-up dressing, butter, cream, lemons and hot tea packets should be on hand for every seated function. I have included a beverage station worksheet in the addendum, which provides guidance for planning your beverage station requirements. All three stations must be placed in such a way that your service staff can drop off dishes, pick up food and replenish beverages, without running into one another. If you can pull off that feat you'll save yourself, your wait staff----and your guests----a lot of confusion.

Chapter 5

Banquet Service

We have so far made our way through four chapters of ideas, suggestions and procedures about how to put together a quality banquet. And we've yet to welcome a single guest! As you can see, many things have to be done well in order for you to have any chance at all of providing excellent service.

Your sales team attracted a client, first of all. They helped the client select a menu. They negotiated the final counts, the time and the place, the layout and the special requests; and eventually got their signature on the contract. Your kitchen staff purchased the food, planned and put together the prep requirements, cooked and dished out the food, while your stewarding department made sure everything was delivered to the right location. Your banquet manager finalized the diagrams and planned the buffet set-up or table sets, figured out how much equipment was needed, made sure it got it to the right location, and set the room precisely as you (and the client) had envisioned it. Meanwhile, the beverage department stocked the bars and put them in position. But you're not ready yet. There are still a few meetings that must take place to be sure everyone knows their lines. Let us backtrack for a few important items before we open the doors.

1. The Captains Meeting

The first order of business on event day should be a meeting with your captains to go over all the details. It is traditional to pass out copies of the Event Orders or Function Sheets. The banquet manager or supervisor should go over every detail of the functions to be sure the captains fully understand the plan for both set-up and service. A properly conducted captains meeting will allow your staff to proceed efficiently without having to stop for more information or instructions. It also enables them to answer any questions from the wait staff or your clients at any time during set-up or serve out.

2. Pre-Meal Meeting

Following the completion of the room set, you will remove all equipment from the floor, including any tray jacks, and usher the captains, with their assigned waiters, into the back aisles. At this time you will conduct your pre-meal meeting with the wait staff. I have always preferred to have the captains conduct their own meetings whenever possible. This helps to legitimize the captain's authority and further enhances the team unit. Occasionally, however, particularly on small functions, a few words of praise and instruction from the Top Dog can make a difference.

3. Order of Service

Every function will have an order of service. For seated meals with presentations and many courses there may be as many as 30 steps involved from the time the doors open until the last guest leaves. If your event is to go off as planned all these steps must be communicated to your service staff in a fashion they can understand, remember and execute.

You should make a chronological list of each step that you expect to take place in a banquet. Look at this example:

Doors open	6:30
Invocation	7:00
Waiters enter the room	7:10
Salads are served	7:10 - 7:40
Entrees are served	7:40 - 8:30
Dessert and coffee	8:30 - 9:00
Waiters clear the room	9:00 - 10:00
Dinner is over	10:00

This simple and straightforward list gives everyone a clear picture of how the banquet should unfold. Of course, some events have more than three courses and numerous client interruptions. Whatever framework you eventually start with, there are many holes which must be filled in when the supervisors and captains relay the details of the order of service to the wait staff.

4. Beverage Service in the Dining Room

Too often, banquet managers overlook the importance of detailing the exact plan for providing beverage service, assuming that any competent waiter knows just when to do what. Always remember that with a banquet you are attempting to serve a large number of people, all at once, with a minimum of servers. Most often, you have one waiter for every 30 people. If this same ratio were adopted in a restaurant operation they'd be out of business in a week. As a manager, you must be sure your wait staff knows what is expected of them and just how they are to pull it off. Let me throw out a few ideas for your consumption.

- Always do a thorough check on your back-up beverages and side items. Guests at a seated meal must have two things to be happy: water and coffee! If you run out of either, you will have problems.

- Plan to have your waiters enter the room with pitchers of ice water or tea, as appropriate.

- Train your staff to pour coffee into the cup at the table, using a side towel to wipe away stray drops. Coffee should be offered generously at all meals.

- Cold beverages are traditionally removed from the table before re-filling.

- Consider the option of pre-setting iced tea when a group has no wine or bar service, or when their history suggests they drink mass quantities of tea.

- For dinner, serve coffee on request only until the entree has been dropped.

- On dinners with short service windows, consider the option of leaving full coffee pots on the tables before pulling the waiters off the floor.

- When full cocktail and/or heavy wine service is required, use a separate service staff to handle these duties.

- Conduct training classes on wine service regularly with all staff members including management.

- Pre-set lemon wedges on a B&B at each table for iced tea.

- Be sure all your waiters understand how your beverage service plan fits in with the overall order of service. If three upstart waiters start pouring coffee and wine with the appetizers, they're liable to start a trend that will bring your service plan to a crawl.

5. Styles of Service

They're a few traditional styles of service that have developed over the years that have certain distinguishing characteristics. Most operations take a few ideas from each when developing their own service standards. Let us briefly examine each of the most common styles.

American

American is a common service style which most guests and banquet operations are familiar with. In this style the meals are plated in the kitchen and served in courses in the dining room. Often, the salad and/or dessert will be pre-set, along with the ice water. As each course is finished, the waiter will remove the guest's plate along with the eating utensil that was used and any side items. With the salad course you should remove the dressing. With the entrée you should remove the breadbasket, the butter and the B&B plate. (Some operations remove the salt-and-pepper shakers as well). By the time dessert is served, there should only be a utensil for the dessert, a spoon for coffee, a coffee cup and ice water. Generally, this style requires serving from the left and picking up from the right, though most contemporary banquet managers are not purists on this point. (In fact, it makes more sense to pick up from the left, since that is where the B&B plate is placed.)

French

The French style of table service is distinguished by its focus on preparing part or all of the meal tableside, in the dining room. Such items as the Caesar salad, Chateau Briand and Bananas Foster are typical of French menu items. A rolling wooden cart called a gueridon is often used to present and prepare the food. Plated entrees are served from the right, all other courses from the left. Beverages are served from the right. All courses are removed from the right. French service can be impressive and distinctive when sold and managed properly, but it requires investments in equipment and training, and clients who are not bound by time restrictions.

Russian

In this style of service, food is prepared in the kitchen and served at the table on large platters called Escoffiers. It is traditional for all the waiters to remove their platter covers in unison, tableside. Tureens are use for soup and special bowls for salads. The Escoffiers are presented to the entire table before serving the individual guests. The waiter serves each guest at the table, moving counter-clockwise, offering portions at their request. Empty plates are placed from the right, moving clockwise, and the food is served from the left. Plates are cleared from the right, going counter-clockwise.

Family Style

Family Style service is marked by the serving of food in bowls and platters set on the table for everyone's consumption, much like you would at home. A family style banquet can make a nice impression with certain groups, or in association with theme-related meals. This style is not commonly used due to its informality.

6. Styles of Service 101: In Conclusion

Ultimately, every catering operation will develop its own style of service based on its own experience and the nature of its client base. Often, you will use parts of two or three styles within one function to meet all the requirements called for by the client. Or perhaps you will have to invent an entirely new approach to solve some unusual demand. In any case, the basics of service remain the same. While it is true that some clients can be extremely picky about the details, it has been my experience that the vast majority of guests at banquets are mostly interested in only a few things: good tasting food served in a timely fashion, at the right temperature, along with attentive beverage service and at least a minimum of attention to removing used china and flatware----basically in that order. It is possible to get so caught up in the more elegant details of fine dining and/or service styles that you can forget what your guests are really most interested in. No one will ever complain about the side from which you placed their filet mignon, as long as it got there hot and properly cooked; and when they needed some ice water or coffee, you were nearby.

Chapter 6

Managing the Beverage Department

A large part of any catering operation is the serving of alcoholic beverages. Almost all firms set up a separate department whose duties are to order, store and serve all liquor, beer, wine and soft drinks, even if it's only one person. Your profit margin on beverages is much higher than your profit margin for food. Thus, the caterer who can promote and manage an aggressive mix of beverage sales----alongside their food sales----will see better results on the bottom line. Alcoholic beverages, however, present many challenges for management that are unique to the product.

1. Storage and Ordering

Beverages should be stored in a secure room with limited access that maintains a consistent temperature (72 or slightly below), year round. You will almost always store your liquor, beer and wine in separate areas of the storeroom, and then sub-categorize within each category. Most firms will break it down a step further and separate their product by type (i.e. vodka, gin, whiskey, red or white wine), and then alphabetize within the type. I have found that with larger liquor or wine lists it is easier to not break your liquor out by type, but to simply organize in alphabetical order from top to bottom. Since some members of your staff will not be totally familiar will all the different types and categories of liquor, you may end up saving yourself valuable time searching for product if everything is in a simple alphabetical system.

Fine wines (particularly reds) should be stored on wine racks. This keeps the cork from drying out and prevents air seepage, both of which can ruin an expensive bottle of wine. With most other wines it is acceptable to store them in the case for a year or more without significant deterioration in the product or the cork. White wines and beer should never be chilled unless you plan to serve them in the near future. Allowing white wine or beer to chill and then return to room temperature damages the integrity of the product.

As with all inventory forms, your beverage inventory form should match precisely the location of your product on the shelf. Since you may have as many as 200 different products, and you will be doing inventories continuously, the simple process of matching your forms to your physical set-up will save you weeks throughout the course of a year. Par levels and vendor names (or codes) should be on the inventory forms to aid in ordering. Ordering will normally be done weekly, based on your par levels and any extraordinary needs for upcoming functions. Remember, when ordering wine that few clients are particular enough to complain when you are forced to substitute one wine for another, particularly if it is late into a function (when everyone has had a glass or two).

2. Setting the Bar

You will have to establish your own standards for setting up your bars. Listed below is a typical example.

Item	Well or House	Call	Premium
Vodka	2	1	1
Gin	2	1	1
Scotch	1	1	1
Whiskey	1	1	1
Rum	1	1	1
Tequila	1	1	1
Baileys			1
Peach Schnapps			1
Kahlua			1
Cognac			1

With certain clients you will need to adjust your basic bar set-up to accommodate their tastes. Some groups will tend to drink a lot more whiskey or scotch than is typical. Others may be heavy beer drinkers; or wine.

Most firms put together the bar set-up in the beverage room, either directly on a rolling bar, into a rolling cart, or in another type of secured container that can be moved to the bar location. You should use a bar inventory form to issue all product and to check-in returns.

3. Equipment

Many different contraptions are manufactured for the making of cocktails. Some of these are useful, some can be definitely nice to have, and still others are totally and utterly useless. It is up to you to decide exactly what your cocktail equipment should be, but some things are essential.

One of the essentials is the cocktail shaker. There are two basic types of shakers available. A European cocktail shaker is usually made out of metal or glass with a metal top. It is basically a container that holds about half a liter, fitted with a top that closes tightly around the upper edges of the container. This top also has a smaller top, usually fitted with a built-in strainer, through which the shaken cocktail is poured. American shakers, however, consist of two cones about the same size. One is often made of glass, and the other is metallic. These cones are held together to form a closed container, and the shaken cocktail is poured from either one. Most American shakers do not have built-in strainers, so if you use an American shaker, using a separate strainer is a good idea.

Measures, also known as jiggers, are also essential. Jiggers are most often made of metal, but glass jiggers are common, as well. The standard measurements of a jigger can vary widely, depending on where you are. A jigger typically has a 1 ¼ ounce side and a 3/4 ounce side.

In addition to the equipment mentioned above, you will find that things like these are nice to have, as well: Ice bucket, jugs, electric blender, bowls. You should also have access to ordinary kitchenware, such as knives, corkscrews, chopping board. You will also need stirrers (also known as swizzle sticks), straws, toothpicks, serviettes and cloths.

4. Glasses

Cocktail glasses come in four different basic types:

- First, there are the glasses known as rocks glasses, also known as tumblers. These glasses are usually short and broad glasses, with straight or slightly sloping sides. They normally hold about 125ml and are used for spirits with ice, fruit juices and short drinks.

- Second, there is the highball glass. These glasses are usually of medium width, and are tall with straight or slightly sloping sides. They normally hold between 200 and 300ml and are used for long drinks with ice.

- Third, the champagne glasses are of two different kinds. The most common, the champagne flute, is a tall and narrow glass with a stem. Champagne flutes have thin-glassed sides, and the long, tapering sides can curve both inward and outward. A champagne flute holds approximately 150ml. The second type of champagne glass is the less-known champagne saucer. The champagne saucer is a broad and shallow glass with a stem. The broadness and shallowness of the glass make the champagne loose its fizz quickly, and the glass is therefore less popular than it once was. It is still, however, in use, and such cocktails as the Margarita use exclusively such glasses.

- Fourth is the group known as cocktail glasses. These are the classic cocktail glasses; stemmed and with sharply sloping sides, making it Y-shaped when seen from the side. The classic cocktail glass holds about 90ml and is best suited for short, strong drinks. In addition to these glasses, some drinks, such as the Pina Colada, have special glasses. Unless you are really serious about mixing your cocktails, you don't really need to buy such glasses. Use glasses you already have instead. There are also other glasses available that will work just fine with cocktails.

5. Mixing a Cocktail

Not all cocktails are made in the same manner. Just as the ingredients may vary, there are several ways in which to mix a cocktail. The most frequently used methods are the following:

- Shaking: The cocktail is mixed by hand in a cocktail shaker. The shaker is first filled three quarters with ice, preferably cubes, as crushed ice will tend to melt and dilute the cocktail. The ingredients are then poured on top of the ice, in order of alcohol content (highest first). When shaking a cocktail, hold the shaker in both hands, one hand on the top and the other supporting the base of the shaker, and shake vigorously. When water has begun condensing on the outside of the shaker, the cocktail is sufficiently chilled, and the cocktail should immediately be strained into the glass. In general, shaking creates a colder cocktail than stirring does, but also a cloudier one.

- Stirring: The cocktail is stirred with a glass or metal rod in a mixing glass, before the cocktail is strained into a glass. As with shaking, crushed ice should not be used, and water condensing on the outside shows that the cocktail is finished.

- Blending: An electric blender is used to mix fruit juices, alcohol, fruit, etc. Blending is an excellent way of mixing ingredients that do not blend easily in any other way. Blend the cocktail till it has reached a smooth consistency. If the recipe requires ice, add crushed ice last, but be careful not to add too much, as the cocktail may be watered down. Blending is a much-disputed method of mixing a cocktail, and in general, blending should be avoided unless the recipe demands it.

- Building: When building a cocktail, the ingredients are poured into the glass in which the cocktail will be served. Usually, the ingredients are floated on top of each other, but occasionally, a swizzle stick is put in the glass, allowing the ingredients to be mixed.

6. Controlling Beverage Costs

While your profit margin is always higher with alcohol sales than with food, it nevertheless presents certain challenges to be sure you are maximizing the profit potential of each dollar in sales.

We all would like to have an unwavering faith in the honesty of our fellow man, but the fact remains: If you don't keep a very close eye on your liquor it will disappear----before, during and after the sale. Your first and foremost duty is to keep your product secure. The beverage storeroom should be a high-security area. If you continuously send unescorted employees to the liquor room you are just inviting theft.

Another tool to manage your product, one that is used by many firms, is the perpetual inventory. This is simply a ledger book that tracks every purchase from a vendor, every issuance to a bartender or bar back, and every return, along with any physical inventories. If you use a computer the process is much faster, though it still takes a degree of diligence to keep it accurate. The idea is to know precisely how much of any product you have on the shelf, at all times. By proper auditing of the perpetual inventory system you should be able to at least reduce the outright theft of product from the shelves.

Several methods are employed to reduce the potential for waste or theft by bartenders during the function. One system uses a cup count system, where the actual cups used are counted against the cash turned in. Another system tracks the beverages issued and returned, counting (or weighing), the bottles----as close as possible----in an attempt to compute how much product was actually served, and therefore, how much cash should be in the bartender's drawer. Some operations use both a cup count and physical inventories to hold bartenders accountable.

In order to manage your pour cost on liquor, most firms require their bartenders to measure out each cocktail with a jigger. Traditional pours are one and a quarter ounces for a regular cocktail and two ounces for a martini or Manhattan. Even with a jigger, your bartenders have a vested interest in over-pouring, and will tend to trail the pour in order to get a few extra drops into the drink. Your best shot at controlling over-pouring is to maintain a visible management presence in the room. There is nothing wrong with stepping in behind a bartender from time to time to give them a hand, or even to take over to give them a quick break. Unscrupulous bartenders tend have their own methodology, and they get nervous when a supervisor gets too close to the action.

7. Bar Service

Like your food service in the dining room, your bar service requires proper attention to the planning and preparation phase prior to the function. A continual challenge for a beverage manager is keeping the beer and white wine properly chilled. It is best, if you have the cooler space, to place your beer and white wine into the cooler overnight. While it takes only about twenty minutes to chill room temperature beer in a tub of ice and water, if just ice is poured over your product it is not likely to chill before your event ends. At many banquets, more than half of the crowd will be beer drinkers, and while they may not be picky about the brand, they do tend to agree on the temperature. Sometimes the difference between a four-star gala and a two-star, also-ran affair boils down to the temperature of the beer.

Bartenders are well paid for the amount of work they do, and it is usually easy to attract plenty of good bartenders. You should try to select bartenders who are efficient, honest and professional, while maintaining the highest of appearance standards. Your local beverage distributors are usually more than happy to provide training seminars concerning any of their products that you carry. Take advantage of this resource. As with all your staff, training should remain a priority.

8. Wine Service at the Table

There are almost as many books about wine as there are about food. It is easy to be intimidated when you tread into these well-squashed grapes. We won't attempt to spill it all out here. But the *fundamentals* of banquet wine service are fairly easy to master, and, for the catering professional, a necessity to understand.

Basically, there are three types of wine: red, white and blush. Within these three types you have varietals (specific grapes such as cabernet sauvignon, or chardonnay) and proprietaries (specific vintners such as

Baron de Phillippe Rothschild or Beaulieu Vineyard). It is tempting to call sparkling wine, or champagne, another type, but in reality champagnes are just white or blush wines with extra carbonation added in the fermentation process (and technically, only sparkling wines bottled in the Champagne region of France can be labeled and sold as Champagne). White Zinfandels, in contrast, are blush wines made from the zinfandel grape variety. The timing of how long the skins of the grape are left in with the pulp has a direct correlation to the color of the wine.

White wines, blushes and champagnes should be served chilled, of course, while red wine should be served at room temperature, if not a couple of degrees below. It is widely accepted to serve a Beaujolais (a fruity French red that actually loses punch with age) at between 64 and 68 degrees.

For a la carte service, an ordered bottle of wine would be presented to the host of the party (or the person who ordered the wine), before serving the rest of the table. The bottle should be cradled in a side towel, with the label presented for approval before allowing the host to sample a meager taste and approve the selection. In banquet service, of course, things move much faster.

Almost always, in a banquet setting, the wine will be opened prior to the guests' arrival. White wines will be in ice buckets, pre-set either on the table or on stanchions tableside, while reds will often be placed on a napkin fold near the centerpiece. When wine is pre-set, it should be the first order of service. Waiters should work their way around the table, offering a glass of the guest's choosing to the ladies, then the gentlemen. Red wine should be filled to half a glass and white wine two thirds. The bottle should be held two inches from the edge of the glass and poured straight into the middle of the glass, being careful to twist the bottle as you pull it up, to prevent spills. The bottleneck should be wiped with a side-towel between pours to prevent stray drops on the table or your guests. It is not necessary to query your guests before re-filling their wineglass. Those who have had enough will indicate so before you pour.

While most guests will not dock you quality points for apprentice wine technique, attentive and polished wine service can provide real flash to any affair, and improve your bottom line in the process.

Chapter 7

Coffee Breaks

A big part of any in-house catering operation is the delivery and set-up of coffee breaks. It can account for a considerable portion of an operation's total sales and an even larger percentage of profit. While the basics of setting up a coffee break seem rather straightforward, setting a break properly---and within time constraints----requires an established methodology. In higher volume operations, where you might be dropping 30 or 40 breaks an hour (many of them with food) you must have a method that keeps the idea of flow in its proper perspective. Let us examine what it takes to win the battle of the break.

1. Establish Standards

Once again, documenting your procedures is an important first step in maintaining consistent quality with your final product. A few simple guidelines can go a long way. You must answer the following questions: Do you set your breaks left to right, right to left, or from the door in? (Or does it depend on how you expect the guests to *flow* through the room?) Where do you place your coffee cups and condiments? Do you place food items before beverages? Are your cups placed before the ice and the beverages after? With china services, how many tray jacks should be set out, and where should they be placed? And the list goes on.

2. Staging

The key to managing a good coffee break operation is staging. By staging, I mean the process of getting all the supplies you need in the right location, stored with some sense of organization, and then working from your BEOs to stage your services well before they are delivered. Coffee breaks are much like room service; you must leave the set-up area without forgetting any item you might need to properly service the BEO requirements. Forgetting something as simple as a spoon for the whipped cream can cost you a round trip to the cage, which could take another 30 minutes. Even worse than forgetting something on your way to the room is running totally out of supplies in the middle of a relentless rush. How can you prevent such a crisis?

Like the art of setting a room, running a busy coffee-break operation is a subtle artistry that requires years of experience to master. Among the skills you need are the abilities to juggle the timing of advance orders with event-day replenishments, keep a close eye on your back-up product and pre-staged supplies, and maintain a feel for where your staff is, and how long it will be before they return. The expediter must supervise the staging of the services to ensure that everything is included on the delivery cart, and line up the carts so they leave toward their destination within your time goals, given all the variables. Toward that end, here are some staging concepts that you might find useful.

- Organize the cage area so that your product flows easily toward where the carts are staged.

- Put together inventory forms (with pars) that match up to your storage locations.

- Always add up your product requirements before a large show or convention and order enough product to easily cover all pre-sold product along with conceivable replenishment needs.

- Pre-stage plenty of sugar bowls, creamers, stir-straws and any china needs on the night before any busy event day.

- Pre-set the service in the room (minus the food and beverages), whenever possible.

- Attach a copy of the BEO to the service carts as you pre-stage services.

- Utilize a supervisor or captain to manage the staging of services. Give them the authority to ensure accuracy and timing.

- While pre-assigning services is a necessity in high-volume operations, you must establish the concept of teamwork *on all deliveries* to be successful.

- Post checklists of supplies needed with each food or beverage menu item.

- Keep a running tally of when each service or replenishment left for delivery, and which waiter made the drop.

3. Set Up

Remember the flow! Setting a good coffee break is often no more complex than remembering that simple phrase. But few catering professionals take the concept as seriously as they should. I am purist on the flow of a coffee break; and for good reason. Guests approach your break with a limited amount of time, and thus, they tend to line up as a group to make their way through the buffet, attempting to garner their small portion of the juice, java, and jelly-donuts, before the seminar resumes. If you've set the condiments before the coffee, then the tango line will come to a screeching halt. Training your staff on your service standards is the easiest way to keep the idea of the flow in mind, but you'll never be able to document every eventuality. At some point your staff must be able to visualize the logical flow of your guests through the coffee break set. Elegant breaks that fall short on the concept of flow are nothing more than an elaborate house of cards, destined to fall apart when the first five guests try to work their way through the maze. Keep an eye out for the following details.

- With hot beverages the flow is always: cups, beverages, condiments.

- With cold beverages the flow is cups, ice, beverage product and condiments.

- Often it makes sense to put your condiments on a separate table.

- Be sure you have a small basket or bowl for trash such as sugar packets and stir straws.

- Be sure you have trashcans set near the end of the break and in other accessible locations.

- With china breaks, always have enough trays and tray jacks set in good locations around the room.

- With larger breaks that serve food and beverages, set your food on a separate table from your beverages.

- Review the timing of your client's break schedule, and apply proper planning to match the number of service lines to the number of guests you expect during the time window.

4. Billing and Replenishments

Heavy-duty coffee service operations tend to churn out some serious paperwork. During a big show you may double your advance orders with replenishments. In such an environment you must develop systems to keep the billing and delivery process manageable.

Your first step must be to develop a chain of authority for the ordering of replenishments. Generally, the sales department is the first link in the event day order chain. The sales associates should confirm the billing method and administrate the information to the required departments (i.e. banquets, kitchen, and beverage). All pertinent information should be taken with the replenishment order, including the time of the order and any special requests. If it is a new order (often called a pop-up) you will need to confirm the exact location and any table requirements. A realistic estimate on the time of delivery is also helpful in easing customer expectations. The replenishment order will either be phoned in to the appropriate operational departments or printed by remote. Under the right circumstances, it makes sense to allow the service staff to replenish product as needed, as long as the client is amenable and you have a reliable system for keeping track of the delivered product.

Once the order reaches operations, it should be queued up with all the other orders in the current queue. One easy system to employ is to simply place the most current order at the bottom of the stack, whether on a desk or on a clipboard. (I prefer a clipboard because it makes it harder to get the paperwork out of order.) You should also have a system for keeping track of when the replenishment order leaves the set-up area. One idea that many operations use is to punch the order on a time clock on the way out. This information is important when dealing with customer complaints and billing disputes, or simply to analyze the efficiency of your replenishment system.

Upon delivery, of course, the replenishment order should be signed and a copy left with the client. Since you will be billing the client for payment of these services, you must be sure that the paperwork flows back to the sales department in a complete and organized fashion. How quickly the whole process is managed might well determined how many orders are placed and how much additional sales you will generate. With coffee being sold at $25 a gallon and up, directing a vigorous replenishment operation can make a big difference on the bottom line.

Chapter 8

Equipment and Supplies

Keeping your equipment and supplies' cost in line is one of the most difficult challenges that any manager faces in the food service business. Equipment and supplies are difficult and time-consuming to inventory, constantly in use at different locations, and subject to breakage, theft, and incidental disposal. In high volume operations equipment runs a thin line between being an expense or an asset.

Most firms give the Executive Chef principal responsibility managing equipment and supplies. Often responsibility for linen and buffet props may be delegated to the Banquet Manager. Large firms may have a Stewarding Manager with his own staff. However the responsibility is broken up, it will be important to your firm's success to play close attention to the many details of this function.

It has been my experience that many operations do not take the job of managing their equipment and supplies as seriously as they should. Too often the focus on reducing labor cost hurts your ability to control equipment costs and maintain proper inventory levels. You should remember that losing equipment, whether through breakage, incidental disposal or theft, cost you not only the purchase price of the items, but additional labor costs associated with trying to set-up and service banquets with insufficient inventory. Inventory shortages with simple items like forks and tongs can make your operation second-rate.

High-volume operations, which may have numerous functions taking place at the same time, are particularly susceptible to service problems related to equipment shortages. In my experiences at the Georgia World Congress Center, the Georgia Dome and the Atlanta Marriott Marquis, all extremely high-volume operations, much of my time and efforts were spent in just trying to get the proper equipment in the right locations so we could set-up and service the banquet.

Like the systems you employ with your food and beverages, equipment should be kept in consistent, organized and logical locations. The process of always returning your equipment to the same spot makes it easier to locate for pulls and greatly speeds up inventories. In the same way (and for the same reasons) equipment and supplies should be secured when access is not needed. Even cheap silverware will walk if given an open door; not to mention real silver.

It is important to establish a par level for each item of equipment that is needed for day-to-day operations. Several variables must be added into the mix to determine optimum pars. In a typical restaurant operation the rule of thumb is 2 1/2 times your seating capacity. In banquets, other variables come into play. You must take a look at the total equipment usage you can expect during peak operations----estimates that can only be ascertained by evaluating your sales history. In large operations the pars may run well into the thousands, particularly for flatware and china. You might, from time to time, even consider renting equipment. When planning for rare, unusually high-volume events, this is often the most profitable option.

Because there is no shortage of purveyors of food service equipment (whether new, used or leased) its a buyer's market. Competitive purchasing can make a difference on the bottom line. You must take into account, however, the fact that your equipment will always break, become lost and get stolen. The sturdiness and availability of your principal stock is an important consideration. I once knew a Vice President who wouldn't purchase any dish that couldn't withstand a brisk flip to the carpet.

Linen bags and laundry carts are a good investment for any operation, for the alternative is the floor, or the trash can. The breakdown of functions are seldom closely monitored and will usually occur at the end of a long shift when staff members are more interested in leaving the property than securing the firm's assets. Providing your staff with an adequate amount of queen marys, dish dollies, speed racks and linen carts improves the odds considerably that your equipment and linen will make it back to the dish room and laundry.

Develop a teamwork approach to the breakdown of functions between your service staff and your stewarding department. You should assign a few key members of the service staff to oversee the recovery of all equipment, supplies and props. Larger firms will schedule a late shift to handle the important job of cleaning and securing equipment. I always appointed a lead captain to oversee the recovery of napkins and tablecloths. Similarly, I would appoint one of more captains to be sure that all props were properly returned to storage and secured. Often, the recovery of salt and pepper shakers, florals, vases, candle holders, sugar bowls, etc. are assigned to one of more selected captains.

It has always been my opinion that spending an extra dollar or two in labor to really control the flow of your equipment and supplies will pay off many-fold in the quality and profitability of your overall operation.

Chapter 9

Off-Premise Catering

Off-premise catering brings into play numerous variables that the in-house caterer does not have to juggle. The simple logistics of transporting raw, prepared or semi-prepared food to a remote site is enough of a challenge to make one think twice. But for many firms, if the operation is well managed, off-premise catering can provide a wealth of profit and exposure. Let's look at some ideas for managing the principal challenges of off-premise catering.

1. Evaluating the Event Site

The first challenge that the off-premise caterer must take on is the evaluation of the remote site. Remote sites can be one of many varieties. Often, the location will be an existing public or private facility that has food service equipment and logistical support within the building or on the grounds. In some cases the site will be a private residence. Occasionally, you be putting on an event with little or no kitchen or storage logistics available. In evaluating any site it is important to make a thorough study of the specific dining space, kitchen capabilities and logistical support that is available. You should make a detailed list of the following, at a minimum:

- Dry storage space
- Refrigeration
- Water
- Ice making and storage
- Cooking equipment – quantities, capacities and qualities
- Warming equipment
- Dishwashing

- Garbage removal

- Ingress and egress to the kitchen and dining areas

- Parking

- Quantities of serving equipment available

- Quantities of tables and chairs available

- Skirting and linen available

- Electrical capacities and locations

- Local rules for hosted events, particularly guest count maximums

By putting together a detailed analysis of the site in document form you will have a ready reference for future events sold at the site. Understanding the space within which you will be working will better enable you to sell an event that makes sense, both for the client and for yourself. You should never hesitate to point out logistical issues that may result from an overly ambitious layout or menu plan. Once again, ideals and realities often do not intersect neatly. Understanding the site also allows you to construct a staffing, preparation and service plan that works in concert with the logistics of the site.

2. Food Preparations and Transportation

The most difficult challenge presented by off-premise catering is the preparation and transportation of the menu items from the kitchen to your remote site. This piece of the planning puzzle must be carefully thought out; experience here means a lot. Here are some good ideas to help you manage the process:

- Cooking and presentation equipment (items such as chafing dishes, pans and bowls) should be carefully counted out based on the menu to be offered. Always add in a buffer for miscalculations and breakage.

- All food preparation that can be done at your home kitchen should be done there. This would include any cutting of any vegetables, meats or garnishes and the making of any sauces that will keep.

- Be sure to label all foods that could be misidentified on site. You don't want to put horseradish sauce on something that calls for a white sauce.

- Prep and seal-wrap all cold trays and sauces at your home kitchen and keep lightly iced or refrigerated until just before serving.

- Similarly, prep and seal-wrap all cold appetizer and salad items and keep cool until just before dish-out.

- Many hot foods – meatballs, for example – will withstand a reasonable length trip in a warming box to the site. Such items may be cooked off before leaving, though remember that they will continue to cook some prior to and subsequent to dish out so back out cooking time appropriately.

- Other hot foods should be prepped and ready for cooking on site.

- Have a detailed plan of how each item will be finished and offered to the service staff for serving or display.

- You should have a timeline of who will perform what function and when.

Not quite as tricky, but certainly critical, is the transport of serving equipment both to and from the remote property. Most off-premise caterers have storage bins and carts designed for the purpose of transporting specific equipment items such as plates, glasses, silverware and buffet pieces. Anything that can break, of course, will, even in a quiet in-house affair, so you must take great care to pack and secure any breakable or damageable service ware. Certainly the securing of the storage bins and carts within the transportation vehicle is of utmost importance. Even the most diligent of drivers can run into unexpected potholes and traffic emergencies. Often, it makes sense to transport your more delicate food and equipment items in the backseat or trunk of a car, perhaps even in someone's lap. In any case, the transportation plan should be well mapped out as a standard function of the planning process for off-premise catering.

Just as you plan the details of transporting your food and equipment to the site, you should also have a detailed plan for how your equipment will return to your home facility. Not the least of these considerations is the possible removal of garbage, soiled linen and dirty equipment or serving ware.

3. Banquet Service at Remote Sites

Many of the same space and planning considerations that are involved in a local event are applicable to an event that is hosted off-premise. One must carefully walk the space and understand the flow of both the guests and your staff through the areas. Make note of nooks and crannies that can be used for back-up storage of supplies, breakdown areas and garbage disposal. Temporary storage areas can be constructed with the use of convention-style piping and curtains. The typical problems that are encountered in off-premise catering mostly revolve around the flow of food into the service area and then back to the breakdown areas. Since you will most often be sharing space with the kitchen staff it is important to map out the aisle ways that your staff will observe during the event.

Chapter 10

Financial Analysis and Making a Profit

Keeping track of the financial aspects of your firm's operation requires the attention of every member of your management staff. Long before you turn the numbers over to your accountant (or accounting department as the case may be), you should have a clear picture of where you stand from a profitability standpoint. Let's start by taking a quick and dirty look at an example of a catering firm that is doing everything right.

1. Financial Statements   Monthly Profit and Loss

Sales		
Item	Dollars	Percentage
Sales	$100,000	100%
Operating Expenses		
Food	28,000	28%
Beverage	10,000	10%
Salaries	10,000	10%
Hourly Wages	12,000	12%
Supplies	5,000	5%
Linens	500	.5%
Sales and Admin	3,000	3%
Utilities	4,000	4%
Total Operating Expenses	72,500	72.5%
Total Operating Profit	27,500	27.5%
Fixed Costs		
Insurance	1,000	1%
Property/Equipment	8,000	8%
Depreciation	500	.5%
Total Fixed Costs	9,500	9.5%
Gross Profit	18,000	18%
Net Income	$10,800	10.8%

Now, obviously, firms will vary greatly on their mix of fixed costs, depending on the nature of their business (in-house or outside catering), the costs associated with their location (hotel, convention, restaurant, or free-standing), and various other considerations related to the rental or purchase of equipment and the cross-utilization of salaried personnel from other profit centers (i.e. restaurants or rooms divisions). Most of these expenses are beyond the control of your catering management staff. Therefore, they must focus their attention on the numbers at the top of the statement. The principal controllable costs (referred to as controllables) are food, beverages, supplies and labor. Let's look at each of these and discuss systems for keeping your costs in line with your sales.

2. Food Cost Analysis

We covered many of the details important to controlling food cost in the chapter on Managing the Kitchen. But how do you know if your hard work is paying off? The principal tool of analysis in the kitchen is the inventory. Within your monthly cost statement you will break down your food cost by category. Most firms use the following: meats (which may be subdivided by type), dry goods, produce, and non-alcoholic beverages. On a monthly basis you will be able to compare your percentage costs to previous months and year-to-date costs. Any unusual jumps in a particular category should be examined carefully. Often in a catering operation (as opposed to a restaurant), your menu mix will have a big impact on how your food cost mix breaks out. If you happen to have sold two big dinners this month, with expensive cuts of meat, you will probably see a jump of a percent or two in your meat cost. Month-to-month variations are to be expected as long as you can maintain your budgeted percentage over the course of the year.

Whenever a new menu is developed, the chef should carefully break out the exact cost of all the food product needed to produce each item, before the final pricing decisions. Include some realistic cushion for waste in this estimate. Experienced caterers will look at each menu item's cost to sales ratio (food cost %) in relationship to the total menu mix, as well as in comparison to the competition. Some of your higher end menu items may run well over 30% cost to produce, while others will run under 20%. A quick examination of your actual menu mix from last year can help you to figure out how much of each item you can expect to sell with the new menu.

In the same way, anytime you sell a menu item that is not from your printed menu selections, your chef should do a quick cost analysis on what it costs to produce one unit of the item. Clearly, there are occasions when it is a good idea to give a client a price break. But if you continually sell menus that don't meet realistic cost-budgeting goals, then you must either reduce your profit goals, or cut back your expenses in other areas.

I've never understood why more operations don't tie in the chef's salary and/or bonuses with food cost. With a firm doing $1,000,000 a year, a 1% reduction in food cost is $10,000. How little of that would you need to funnel to the chef to keep him or her focused on the goal?

3. Labor Cost

Your second largest expense is the cost of labor. Keeping your labor costs at or below budgeted levels is a challenge every banquet manager must take on daily, with sense of purpose; and a plan. Just as you analyze the costs associated with your menu items, you should project and analyze the labor costs associated with specific events or shows. The easiest way to control labor is to schedule only as many people and hours as your budget allows.

Such an approach, of course, requires some tricky cost analysis and, occasionally, even trickier service strategies. The process works something like this:

Projected sales for Johnson dinner	$20,000
Budgeted labor allowance @12%	1,200
Divided by Average Rate @ $10.00	120 Available Hours
Divided by total time needed to set and service the room	8 Hours
Equals number of service staff to schedule and still be within budget allowance	15

This is the easiest way to plan your labor requirements on a function by function basis. As long as you have a labor percentage determined for each department, your management staff can use their budget to compute the amount of staff they should schedule. Obviously, in the real world, staffing needs don't always match up exactly with your budget. For large receptions, for example, you should generally run a labor percentage that is much lower than you budget. For large seated meals (particularly with long breaks), service requirements will tend to push your labor cost per dollar to the higher side.

We have used the service staff as an example here, but each department must have its own budget, and use similar analysis to plan employee schedules. If you're doing only four events a week, it might make sense to break out your analysis on an event-to-event basis. If you're a hotel or convention center you might want to complete your projections and recaps weekly. Then intent is to match your labor dollars spent to your actual sales, and react when your percentages are not where they should be.

Chapter 11

Cleaning Up

I once heard a story about a pilot who performed an amazing feat by landing a passenger plane after it had been critically damaged in a thunderstorm. Having lost almost all his controls, he used only his tail rudder to guide the plane down through the clouds to safety. As the pilot exited the plane he noticed all the passengers were still standing on the tarmac, staring up at the plane in amazement.

"How did you do it?" they asked him, to which he shrugged modestly.

"But look!", one of them asked, pointing to the craft. "Both wings have fallen off!"

The pilot looked back at the plane and shook his head.

"Details," he muttered, "details."

Hopefully, none of us will ever have to land a plane that has lost both its wings; or even fly one through a thunderstorm. Fortunately, most jobs in this world are not quite that complex. But you may find yourself (if you stay in the catering business for any length of time) battling challenges that seem as unstable and unpredictable as thunderstorms, and you may wonder why you put yourself in the pilot's seat.

Few businesses challenge the full range of a manger's skill like the catering business. From an intimate, gourmet dinner for a select group, to a reception for several thousand, every event tests your ability to plan, communicate and lead. In the end, the difference between you and the competition comes down to details. Grand schemes and concepts are merely dreams. It is the ability to deliver quality food and attentive service that is the meat and potatoes of catering. To pull that off you must have a plan.

Addenda

Sales Event Checklist

1. ___ Copy of client's itinerary or program
2. ___ Exact times on door's opening, speeches, and presentations
3. ___ How are guests arriving?
4. ___ Parking requirements
5. ___ Coat check requirements
6. ___ Other client functions before or after event
7. ___ Schedule of set-up and rehearsal for entertainment
8. ___ Catering needs for entertainment, volunteers
9. ___ How are any client tickets being administered?
10. __ Seating and service requirements of VIP's, or head table
11. __ Room layout and diagrams reviewed and approved by client
12. __ Did client sell their tables with their own numbering scheme?
13. __ Vegetable plates or other special dietary requirements
14. __ Guarantee and Set
15. __ Contracts signed
16. __ Billing procedures explained
17. __ Authorized signatories

SAMPLE MENU
DINNER, BANQUET, AND WEDDING MENU

APPETIZERS

Fresh Vegetable Display $1.25 pp.

Fresh Seasonal Fruit Display $2.25 pp.

Assorted Cheese Display with Baked Goods and Crackers $1.50 pp.

Honesty's Famous Barbecued Meatballs $2.00 pp.

Buffalo Wings $1.75 pp.

Grilled Chicken Kabobs with Peppers and Onions $2.75 p.p.

Honey Mustard Wings $1.55 pp.

BBQ Wings $1.75 pp.

Teriyaki Wings $1.75 pp.

Spicy Pork Meatballs $2.00

Thinly Sliced Tenderloin of Beef with Horseradish Sauce and Assorted Mini Rolls $6.95 pp.

Spinach in Puff Pastry $2.00 pp.

Rumaki (Chicken Liver in Bacon) $2.00 pp.

Goose Liver Pate with Assorted Crackers $2.00 pp.

Sesame Chicken with Honey Mustard Sauce $1.75 pp.

Tomato Tart $1.75 pp.

Tortilla Rounds $1.75 pp.

Curry Chicken with Walnuts in Puff Pastry $3.00 pp.

Chicken Salad in Mini Rolls $2.00

Caribbean Beef or Vegetable Patties $2.00 pp.

Assorted Mini Sandwiches $2.00 pp.

Chicken Satay on with Peanut Dipping Sauce $2.00 pp.

Stuffed Cherry Tomatoes $1.50 pp.

Snow Peas Stuffed with Herbed Cheese $1.50 pp.

Hot Stuffed Mushroom Caps $1.50 pp.

Assorted Mini Rolls $.60 pp.

SEAFOOD APPETIZERS

Salmon Mouse on Toast Wedges $2.00 pp.

Crab Balls $2.50 pp. Hot Crab Dip $3.00 pp.

Smoked Trout Chevrons on Crackers with Horseradish Cream $2.50 pp.

Whole Salmon Stuffed with Crabmeat $6.95 pp. (min. 20)

Scallops Wrapped in Bacon $2.50 pp.

Iced Jumbo Shrimp with Cocktail Sauce (2) $3.00 pp. Shrimp Tree Additional $100.00

Large Shrimp with Cocktail Sauce (2-3) $2.50 pp.

Mini Crab filled Tartlets $2.50 pp.

Jumbo Mushroom Stuffed with Crab $2.25 ea./pp.

Large Spiced, Grilled, or Garlic Shrimp $2.50 pp.

Shrimp Kabobs with Peppers and onions $3.75 pp

OTHER APPETIZERS

Herbed Cheese on Endive $1.25 pp.

Prosciutto Ham with Melon, $2.50 pp.

Blue Cheese Spread with Walnuts on Crudettes $1.75 pp.

Mini Spinach & Cheese Quiche $2.00 pp.

Large Chocolate Covered Strawberries $3.00 ea. (seasonal, market priced)

Chocolate Covered Driscoll Stemmed Strawberries $3.50 ea. (seasonal, market priced)

Strawberry Tree, Includes Assorted Cheeses, Fruit, and Fresh Vegetable Display $400.00 feeds 100 (seasonal, market priced)

Sausage in Puff Pastry $2.00 pp.

Mixed Nuts $12.50 per lb.

Assortment of Dry Snacks $1.75 pp.

ENTREES

Smoked Turkey $5.50 pp.

Roasted Beef $7.25 pp.

Steamship Round $400.00

Meat Carver $150.00 for 3 hours (with Steamship Round)

Tenderloin of Beef $14.00 pp.

Prime Rib of Beef $14.00 pp.

Roasted Turkey $4.25 pp.

Honey Baked Turkey $6.50 pp.

Roasted Turkey Breast $4.75 pp.

Fried or Baked Chicken $3.50 pp.

Stuffed Chicken Breast $10.00 pp.

Baked Chicken Breast $5.25 pp.

Grilled Chicken Breast $6.25 pp.

Jerked Chicken Breast $7.00 pp.

Baked Ham $4.25 pp.

Honey Baked Ham $6.50 pp.

Barbecued Spare Ribs $7.50 pp.

Whole Salmon Stuffed with Crabmeat $7.95 pp. (min. 20)

Crab Stuffed Jumbo Shrimp $11.95 pp.

Authentic New Orleans Ham, Sausage, and Shrimp Jambalaya $9.99 pp.

African Jollof Rice with Chicken or Beef $6.95 pp. without Meat $3.95 pp.

Broiled or Grilled Salmon or Tuna Steak $12.00 pp.

Seafood Newburg $7.95 pp.

Grilled, Broiled Trout or Flounder $6.95 pp. With Crab Stuffing $9.95 pp.

Fried Whiting $3.50 pp.

Gullah Vegetable Paella $3.75 pp.

Vegetarian Lasagna $8.95 pp. (min 10)

Meat Lasagna $6.95 pp. (Min 10)

Cold Sesame Noodles $2.50 pp.

Spaghetti with Meat Sauce $4.50 pp.

Bowtie Pasta with Smoked Salmon and Dill 7.95 pp.

Pasta Primavera $3.50 pp.

Linguini with Clam Sauce $5.75 pp.

Linguini with Roasted Plum Tomato Sauce $4.75

Spinach Fettuccine with Chicken in Spicy Tomato Sauce $6.75 pp.

SIDE DISHES

Green Beans, Peas, Buttery Corn, Grilled Tomato $2.00

Grilled Eggplant, Zucchini, Mushrooms, Red or Yellow Sweet Bell Pepper $2.25

California Medley of Broccoli, Cauliflower, and Baby Carrots $2.00

Herbed Stuffing, Yams, Sweet Potato Soufflé, Broccoli $2.50 pp.

Mother's Potato Salad $2.50 pp

Roasted Red Bliss Potatoes $2.00

Homemade Mashed or Scalloped Potatoes $2.50 pp.

Rice $1. 50 pp. Rice Pilaf $2.00 pp.

Baked Sweet Potato, Baked White Potatoes $2.00

Fresh Collard Greens, Turnips or Kale $2.50 pp.

Garden Salad with Dressings $1.25 pp.

Jalapeno Corn Muffins $1.00 pp.

Corn Muffins $1.00 pp.

Assorted Mini-Rolls $1.00 pp.

Golden Dinner Rolls with Butter $1.00 pp.

Fresh Baked Rolls $1.25 pp.

Fresh Baked Bread Loaves - Serves 6 $3.00

BEVERAGES

Iced Tea $2.00 pp. (2 Servings)

Lemonade $2.50 pp. (2 Servings)

Red Punch $1.50 pp. (2 Servings)

Red Punch with Ginger Ale $2.00 pp. (2 Servings)

Fruited Punch $2.50 pp. (2 Servings)

Sparkling Cider Toast $2.00 pp. with 1 refill $2.50 pp.

Fresh Brewed Coffee and Decaf $1.00 pp. with Herbal Tea Service $1.50

Assorted Soda and Sparkling Water $1.15 pp.

DESSERTS

Assorted Cheesecake $3.50 pp.

with Cherries or Strawberries $4.50 pp.

Apple Spiced Cake $3.50 pp. (min. 16)

Carrot Cake $4.50 pp. (min. 16)

Old Fashioned Red Velvet Cake $4.50 pp. (min 16)

Chocolate Mousse $4.50 pp.

Strawberries with Whipped Cream $3.75

Black Forest Cake $4.50 pp. (min 16)

Cherry Crunch $3.75 pp. (min 18)

Apple Pie $3.50 pp.

Homemade Peach Cobbler $5.00 pp.

Homemade Banana Pudding $4.25 pp.

Iced Sheet cake: Vanilla or Chocolate $1.50 pp. (min 30)

Brownies $1.50 pp.

Any Dessert A la mode add $1.50 pp.

Assorted Sherbet $1.50 pp.

French Pastries $2.50 pp.

Large Chocolate Covered Strawberries $3.50 ea.

Chocolate Covered Driscoll Stemmed Strawberries $4.50 ea.

Assorted Cookies $1.25 pp.

Wedding Cake $3.00 pp. plus Accessories and Delivery

Job Description - Banquet Captain

Qualifications

- At least three years of experience in banquets, with some lead or supervisory experience
- Good communication skills
- Good administrative skills

Job Duties

- Be able to understand and implement standard operating procedures
- Be able to read and evaluate Banquet Event Orders
- Be able to devise room sets for smaller functions, including table placement, food locations and decor
- Be able to delegate job assignments to catering wait staff
- Be able to train catering wait staff
- Be able to oversee banquet functions to maximize service and profitability

Wave Set
Captain's Assignments

Event _____   Date/Time
                                          _____

Location   Lead Captain
_____   _____

Captain	Color/Code	Assignment
Rodney	Blue	Forks, B&B's
Frank	Black	Knives, Spoons, Cups, Saucers
Pat	Orange	Florals, Sugar Bowls, S&P, Creamers, Dressing, Butter
Will	Purple	Head Table
Chet	Silver	Pre-Set Wine
Mary	White	Service Aisle
All		Drop Salads, Desserts, Water

Beverage Station Worksheet

Function _____

Location _____

Date/Time _____Number of Stations _____
Assigned to _____

Ice Water:　set count _____ x .06 = ____ gallons　per station = _____
Iced Tea:　set count _____ x .06 = ____ gallons　per station = _____
Coffee:　　set count _____ x .06 = ____ gallons　per station = _____
Decaf:　　　set count _____ x .02 = ____ gallons　per station = _____
Hot Water: set count _____ x .005 = ____ gallons　per station = _____
Ice: set count _____ x .001 = _____ ice bins　per station = _____
Coffee Pots:　set count _____ /30 = _____ x 2 = _____
　/(#stations) = _____
Water Pitchers:　count _____ /30 = _____ x 2 = _____
/(#stations) = _____
All stations to have the following:
_____1.　Back up sugar, sweet and low and equal
_____2.　Back up cream
_____3.　Hot tea pitchers
_____4.　Hot tea packets
_____5.　Lemons
_____6.　Back up dressing
_____7.　Back up butter

Additional table diagrams, buffet sets and other addenda are available at:

http://www.cateringcomplete.com

Printed in the United Kingdom
by Lightning Source UK Ltd.
104036UKS00001B/36